THE MENTAL NIGHTMARES-HORRORS AND PAIN FROM TAKING CHOLESTEROL MEDICINE

THE MENTAL NIGHTMARES-HORRORS AND PAIN FROM TAKING CHOLESTEROL MEDICINE

MEDICINE HORRORS

KENNY B

authorHOUSE®

AuthorHouse™
1663 Liberty Drive
Bloomington, IN 47403
www.authorhouse.com
Phone: 1-800-839-8640

Published by AuthorHouse   03/20/2012

ISBN: 978-1-4634-0722-3 (sc)
ISBN: 978-1-4634-0720-9 (hc)
ISBN: 978-1-4634-0721-6 (e)

Library of Congress Control Number: 2011908605

INTRO

IS THIS
MEDICINE KILLING ME??

- THIS BOOK IS ABOUT THE MEDICINE I TOOK AND THE AFFECTS OF NOT ONLY MY HEALTH, BUT MENTAL AND THE WAY I HAD TO WORK AROUND THE TROUBLES AND SIDE AFFECTS, THE TYPE OF WORK! I HAD TO STAY WITH, HOW YOU FEEL GOING TO WORK, THE WORRY NOT KNOWING WHATS GOING ON WITH YOUR BODY AND THE DOCTOR AT TIMES NOT HELPING BY SAYING THERE'S NOTHING WRONG, AT LEAST AT TIMES THE BLOOD WORK DIDN'T SHOW ANY THING.

- TELLING THE PEOPLE WHO READ THIS BOOK THAT IF THEY MAY HAVE A SIMILAR PROBLEM, TO LET THEM KNOW YOU AND ONLY YOU KNOW HOW YOU FEEL WHEN YOU ARE FEELING GOOD FOR 45 YEARS, AND THE DOCTOR TELLS YOU NOW TAKE THIS DRUG IT WILL MAKE YOU BETTER AND LIVE LONGER? NOTICE IF YOU FEEL BETTER, WORSE, OR IF LUCKY, NO PROBLEMS OR SIDE AFFECTS.

- QUESTION MARK?, WILL IT REALY HELP YOU LIVE LONGER OR THE SIDE AFFECTS NOW CONTROL YOUR LIFE, OR BRING YOUR LIFE DOWN WEAKEN YOUR BODY, CAUSE CANCER, OR OTHER. THE MENTAL HEALTH IS HORRIBLE IF YOU GO THROUGH WHAT I DID, I KNOW!!!!!!

- I ALSO KNOW OF MANY OTHER PEOPLE, WHO HAD THE SAME TROUBLES AND THE DOCTOR TOLD THEM SOME OF THE SAME THINGS MINE DID. NOT IN SO MANY WORDS BUT ITS IN YOUR MIND, THERES NOTHING WRONG, YOUR BREATHING TROUBLE IS IN YOUR MIND. YOUR ACHES AND PAIN, JOINT PAIN, <u>STOMACH ULCER</u>, AND OTHER THINGS.

1

- WELL I LET MY DOCTOR KNOW, I WENT TO HIM FOR ABOUT 3 YEARS AT THE TIME OF THIS MESS
- MAYBE MORE AND WHEN I GOT ON THE DRUGS MY HEALTH CHANGED OVER TIME, OVER NIGHT DID HAVE THE ELECTRIC SHOCKS IN BRAIN, DIDN'T KNOW THIS WAS PART OF THE MEDICINE AFFECTS.
- WHEN I RUN OUT OF THE MEDICINE I GOT BETTER, A 5 YEAR OLD KID COULD FIGURE THAT OUT. WHAT EVER THIS IS, IT GETS ME SICK!.
- BUT YOU ALWAYS STICK TO WHAT THE DOCTOR SAYS, AT LEAST FOR A WHILE LIKE I DID. WHEN I WOULD SAY THATS IT CAN'T TAKE THAT PILL, HE WOULD GIVE THE NEXT ONE ON THE LIST OF CHOLESTEROL MEDS. MY DOCTOR FROM CHILDHOOD HAD DIED, THE OTHER DOCTORS ARE VERY GOOD DOCTORS BUT SOMETIMES THEY DON'T LISTEN AT FIRST. I WAS TOLD THAT SOME TEST THE DOCTOR SAID THEY DON'T HAVE THE RIGHT STUFF FOR TESTING. AND I DIDN'T HAVE THE RIGHT AMOUNT OF MONEY BEING MADE TO GET OTHER HELP AT THAT TIME.
- I WILL TRY TO LIST THE ORDER THINGS HAPPENED BUT, THIS IS OVER ABOUT 5 YEARS AND SOME STUFF SEEM TO OVERLAP, THANKS HOPE THIS HELPS IN ANY WAY. THIS BOOK IS ALSO A QUESTION MARK? OF WHY THIS HAPPENS SO OFTEN? WHY ARE SO MANY DRUGS OUT THERE THAT OFFER SO MUCH SIDE AFFECTS FOR SOME DRUGS IN THE OLD DAYS, I THINK THEY WERE CONTROLLED BETER. THE DRUG I WAS ON WAS GIVEN FIRST, DON'T REMEMBER ANYONE SAYING THIS FOOD IS HIGHER IN CHOLESTEROL THAN THAT ONE. STAY AWAY FROM IT WHEN YOU CAN. TRY THIS FIRST BEFORE YOU TAKE MEDICINE. YOU WILL THANK ME.
- THIS BOOK ALSO TELLS YOU WHY HEALTH CARE IS HIGH, ITS NOT ALWAYS THE BODY GIVING UP AND GETTING SICK, SOMETIMES THERES HELP ON THIS, FOODS AND MEDICINE, FOOD'S HAVE THINGS YOU DON'T THINK OF IN THEM. YOU EAT WHAT THE COWS ARE FED, AND SO ON. I NOW USE ORGANIC MILK WHEN I CAN. ALSO IT SEEMS TO LAST LONGER. TOMATOES HOME GROWN WITH NO PESTICIDES, FOOD IN A CAN OR OTHER, IF I AM FEELING GOOD AND EAT CANNED

ANY THING, AND DON'T FEEL RIGHT AFTER, I MAKE A NOTE, NEXT TIME I EAT IF DOES THE SAME
- I WILL NOT EAT IT AGAIN!

I STAY AWAY FROM M.S.G. WHEN I KNOW ITS IN SOMETHING. SOME COMPANYS ARE TAKING M.S.G OUT OF THERE PRODUCTS. AT LEAST I MAJOR SOUP COMPANY SAID THEY WOULD. I HAD SAW SOMEWHERE THAT THIS WOULD HAPPEN. THERE MUST BE A REASON, IF MORE PEOPLE ARE HAVING TROUBLE WITH THIS STUFF.

THIS BOOK IS MOSTY ABOUT MY LIFE OF WHAT HAPPENED AFTER TAKING CHOLESTEROL MEDICINE. AND HOW MEDICINES CAN BRING YOUR LIFE DOWN, KILL YOU, AND MAKE YOU JUST SUFFER WITH PAIN, HORROR OF NOT KNOWING WHAT YOU WILL DO FROM DAY TO DAY.

NO ONE KNOWS THERE TIME HERE ON EARTH, AND YOU NORMALY DON'T THINK OF IT, WHEN THE ODDS CHANGE THAT MAKE IT SOONER TO DIE, OR YOU THINK ITS SOONER, ITS A MENTAL NIGHTMARE! AND IT CONTROLS YOUR LIFE.

LOOK UP THE INFO AND SIDE AFFECTS ON YOUR MEDICINE ON THE NET & THE SIDE EFFECTS YOU'LL SEE, AND MAYBE HORROR STORYS LIKE MINE AND MORE. MAYBE EVEN A STORY LIKE YOUR OWN.

PLEASE NOTE I HAD TO REMOVE THE REAL NAMES OF THE MEDS FOR NOW, IF I FIND OUT I DO HAVE CANCER I WILL RELEASE LATER, BUT ALL ARE BIG NAMES, I WILL SEND THE REAL NAMES TO ALL DOCTORS WHO ASK, AND FDA, AND WILL SEND WASHINGTON A COPY, ALSO LOCAL STATE CAPITAL, AFTER ALL THEY PAID FOR SOME OF MY CARE WHEN I COULD NOT, BUT SOME BIG DOGS IN THE GOV. HAD TO SAY OK TO RELEASE THE DRUG, I'AM THE ONE WHO IS STILL SUFFERING AND OTHERS LIKE ME, MY KIDNEYS ARE HURTING TODAY, DEC.25,2011.

KEN

THE LIST!

HERES A LIST OF SOME OF THE TROUBLES FROM CHOLESTEROL MEDICINE, AND THE OTHER MEDS I TOOK TO COUNTER-REACT THE SIDE AFFECTS.

1. ANXIETY
2. BLOOD SUGAR LEVELS
3. HARD TO FIND BLOOD IN ARM? WITHIN A YEAR THE NURSE NOTICED THE SAME AS WHAT I'VE BEEN SAYING, STRINKING OF VEINS SEEN SOME WHERE WHY USE?)
4. HARD TO BREATHE
5. CAN'T TAKE THE HEAT, MORE SENSITIVE TO HEAT (GETS ME WEAK FAST)
6. STROKE? HEART ATTACT?—WHEN ON BRAND—VX
7. KIDNEY PROBLEMS, AND TEST TAKEN
8. BRAND—RG & TROUBLE
9. MUSCLES ACHES, AND NOW WEAK MUSCLES
10. JOINT ACHES, (NOW SEEM TO BE PERMENENT)
11. PAINS ALL OVER, AND SOME TIMES IN SAME AREA
12. WARTS ON FEET—LEFT WHEN GOT OFF THE DRUGS
13. CANCER SPOTS ON SKIN, ARMS AND OTHER PLACES
14. RED SPOT ON SKIN—STEVEN JOHNSON SYNDROME?
15. LOST OF WORK & THE PAIN I SUFFERED
16. MENTAL OF THE WHOLE THING, NOT KNOWING
17. WEARD EAR ACHE & EYE TOGETHER & OTHER
18. RUSH TO HOSPITAL HEART ATTACK?
19. SKIN RASHS—RED ON FACE AND OTHER PLACES
20. CONSTATELY CONSTIPATED & STILL HAVE TROUBLES
21. I PILL PUT ME ON OTHERS
22. HIGH CK LEVELS IN BLOOD—MUSCLE ACHES
23. LOST OF TEETH AND WHY DIDN'T WANT TO SEE DENIST

24. BREAKING DOWN IN SWEAT IN SHOPPING LINE, WANT TO PASS OUT
25. STOMACH BLEEDING MANY TIMES, PASSED OUT AT STORE IN LAFAYETTE
26. COST OF AMBULANCE & HOSPITAL VISIT OUT OF TOWN STILL PAYING FOR AMBULANCE AT THIS TIME.
27. LOST A CHANCE OF A $300.00+ DOLLAR A DAY JOB, AND THE 150.00 A DAY JOB, ASK TO GET OFF DUE TO TROUBLES (WHILE ON BRAND—RG)
28. BLADDER TROUBLES—AND OTHER SIDE TROUBLES (UNDER KIDNEY)
29. ED—WORSE THAN EVER
30. BLOOD RED EYES FROM ANTI ACID MEDS.
31. ALMOST FELL, LOST FEELINGS IN ONE LEG HAPPEN FEW TIMES
32. LEGS WOULD BE STIFF WHEN WAKE UP AND JOINTS WOULD HURT MOST ALL DAY (JOINT PAIN BECAME PERMANENT)
33. HEAD FELT LIKE LIGHTING OR LITTLE ELECTRIC SHOCKS
34. STARTED SHAKING, TREMORS
35. STOMACH BURNING WITH HURT, I HAVE A BAD ULCER
36. MORE SENITIVE TO SMOKE & OTHER THINGS
37. BEE STING—HAD REACTION
38. REACTION TO PAIN MEDICINE—BRAND—TL RUSHED TO HOSPITAL
39. BLOOD IN URINE ALL THE TIME
40. MOOD CHANGES—KILL MY SELF?
41. CHEST PAINS—MORE PICKING ABOVE CENTER LEFT SIDE NEAR ARM /SHOULDER AREA
42. TWITCHING FACE / EYE (WHEN ON BRAND—RG)
43. IN VOLENTARY ARM MOVEMENT WHEN SLEEPING WAKE UP WITH ARM BEHIND MY HEAD & HURTING
44. WEAKNESS—A LOT!! STILL HAVE TO THIS DAY NOV.23, 2011!
45. FLOATERS IN EYE & TURNED YELLOW FEW TIMES ALSO SKIN TURNED YELLOW FEW TIMES

46. **HAD TREMORS FOR A WHILE, BELIEVE WHEN ON THE BRAND—RG, HAVEN'T HAD IN A WHILE.**
47. **NECK WOULD SOUND LIKE SAND WAS IN IT AFTER ABOUT THE FIRST YEAR, GRINDING NOISE**
48. **BACK & LEGS—LOST BALANCE FEW TIMES**
49. **PASSED OUT AT WORK, LAIDED ON FLOOR FOR WHILE**
50. **HEART RACING, WHILE IT WASN'T? ALSO HEART FELT LIKE IT WAS JUMPING AROUND IN MY CHEST, VERY WORRYED WHEN THIS HAPPENED.**
51. **THE COURT ADVENTURE**
52. **FIBROMYALGIA—WAS TOLD I HAD FROM ALL THIS**
53. **CAN'T BORROW MONEY—MEDICIAL COLECTIONS**

THERE ARE ALSO THINGS I DIDN'T COVER IN BOOK, BONE PAINS, TENDON PAINS AND A NEW DRUG USED NOT LONG AGO GIVE EVEN MORE HORRORS, AND PAIN FOR OVER 4 MONTHS AND DON'T SEEM TO BE LEAVING.

I HAD TO TAKE OUT THE REAL NAMES IN THE BOOK, BUT I TOOK, MANY NAME BRAND DRUGS, AND DO STILL HAVE HEATH TROUBLE BECAUSE OF THESE AND THE LAST BLOOD PRESSURE MED THAT MADE MY INSIDES FEEL LIKE THEY WHERE ON FIRE, I STILL HAVE STOMACH TROUBLE TODAY, MARCH 28, 2012, AS OF THIS LAST EDIT.

KENNETH BOYNE

MEDICINE HURT OR HELP?

ALL MY MEDICAL TROUBLES, ME OR SOMEONE ESE? PERFECTLY HEALTHY GUY MID 30S WORKING OFFSHORE FOR MANY YEARS, ONE DAY AT THE DOCK, THE BOAT I WAS ON WAS BUMPED, I WHEN SLIDING DOWN SOME STEEP STAIRS, I WOKE UP A FELLOW EMPLOYEE FROM THE NOISE. WELL I HAD TROUBLE WITH MY BACK, LATER SLID ON SOME PLATES THAT MOVED, I ENDED UP WITH A SLIPPED DISK OR HURNIADED DISK. I WAS TOLD TO LOSE WEIGHT IT WOULD HELP. I WENT ON A LIQUID DIET, THE DIET YOU GET ONLY WITH A DOCTOR, ALONG WITH MY OWN DOCTOR. WITHIN ONLY ABOUT 2 WEEKS, I LOST WEIGHT, BUT I ENDED UP ON BLOOD PRESURE MEDICINE. I AM ADDING IN TODAY I FOUND OUT SOMETHING ESE OF THE PAST TROUBLES WHILE ON THE DIET, I DRANK A LOT OF DIET DRINKS AND HAD SOME TROUBLE WITH MY STOMACH, DOCTOR SAID GET OFF, I HAD FOUND OUT TODAY THE SWEETENER USED IN MOST DIET DRINKS IS VERY BAD STUFF, AND CAUSES A WHOLE LOT OF MEDICIAL PROBLEMS. LOOK ON YOUR DIET DRINK FOR THE NAME, THEN LOOK UP ON THE NET WHAT SOME DOCTORS SAY, AND WHY GREED ALOWED TO BE LEFT ON THE MARKET, MONEY. MY HEALTH THEN AND NOW WAS CONTROLED BY MONEY AND GREED. I FELT SICK WHEN I READ WHAT I DID, AND PEOPLE DON'T ALL KNOW ABOUT ITS SIDE AFFECTS.

THIS QUESTION IS TO THE F.D.A. WHO I TRYED TO GET IN CONTACT WITH MANY TIMES, NOT ONE PERSON CALLED OR WROTE TO ME. WHY DID PEOPLE HAVE TO GO TROUGHT THOSE TROUBLES OF DIET DRINKS, AND THE CHOLESTEROL MEDICINES? WHY? I WISH MY DAD KNOWN ABOUT THE DIET DRINKS, SOUNDED LIKE SOME OF THE THINGS HE HAD HAPPEN TO HIM JUST BEFORE HE DIED, HE COULD NOT SEE,

HE TOLD ME ONE TIME HIS SUGAR WAS OUT OF CONTROL AT TIMES, HE HURT ALL OVER AND NO ONE KNEW WHY, HE TALKED ABOUT LIGHT FLASHS, TUNNEL VISION AT TIMES, A FEW TIMES HIS SUGAR WOULD DROP BAD, WAS THIS THE DIET DRINK? HE DRANK A LOT OF DIET DRINKS AND USED THE DIET SUGARS. ONE OF MY AUNTS DOCTORS TOLD HER DON'T USE FAKE SUGAR, REAL SUGAR WAS SAFER, THIS MUST HAVE BEEN SOMETHING HE KNEW WAY BACK THEN, ABOUT MID 80S I WOULD SAY THIS WAS SAID, SORRY I'AM FINDING OUT THINGS THAT I ALSO WISH I NEW BEFORE I TOOK. PLEASE GO TO THESE SITES, JUST LOOK UP DIET SWEETENERS AND SIDE AFFECTS. I HOPE YOU DON'T GET SICK AFTER READING.

BACK TO ME, THIS WAS A SIDE AFFECT OF TAKING THE WEIGHT LOST PROGRAM FOR ME SOME OF THE ABOVE. I TOOK MEDICINE AND STILL TAKE TODAY. BY THE WAY ITS A FACT, A HIGH PERCENT OF PEOPLE WHO WERE ON THE <u>LIQUID DIET</u>, ENDED UP ON BLOOD PRESURE MEDICINE. ALL THESE YEARS COST ME MONEY BECAUSE OF A PRODUCT THAT WAS NOT SAFE, AT LEAST IN MY EYES AND I'AM SURE ANY ONE ON BLOOD PRESURE MEDS WOULD SAY THE SAME. I KNOW 2 OTHER PEOPLE IN MY OWN FAMILY THAT TOOK THE <u>LIQUID DIET</u> AND LIKE ME ENDED UP TAKING BLOOD PRESURE MEDS. THIS WAS A DIET PROGRAM AND WAS ON TV I BELIEVE 20/20, IT TALKED ABOUT THE HIGH PERCENT OF PEOPLE ON BLOOD PRESURE MED AFTER GETTING ON THE DIET. I SAW BUT DIDN'T REMEMBER UNTILL TO LATE.

THE DOCTORS THAT I SAW FOR MY BACK, ONE WANTED TO OPERATE, THE DOCTOR IN LAFAYETTE, LA. WANTED TO CUT ME RIGHT OFF THE BAT. THE DOCTOR IN NEW ORLEANS SAID THE DISK DID NOT BUST I COULD LIVE WITH OUT THE OPERATION, REMEMBER I WAS HURT AT WORK AND HAD TO GET A LAWYER INVOVLED, I DIDN'T WANT TO BUT A FEW FELLOW WORKERS TOLD ME I SHOULD, OR WOULD GET FIRED. I LIKED WORKING OFFSHORE AND JUST WANTED MY BACK AND LIFE BACK. WELL THE LAST TIME I WENT TO THE DOCTOR IN LAFAYETTE. HE HAD BEEN CALLED UPON BY THE

BOAT COMPANYS LAWYER, I WAS TOLD THEY SAID IF HE OPERATED THEY WOULD NOT PAY FOR THE OPERATION. THIS CHANGED HIS VIEW BECAUSE HE TOLD ME NOW I DON'T NEED THE SURGERY AND HAD A WHOLE DIFFERENT ATTITUDE. I AM GLAD HE CHANGED HIS MIND, OR SHOULD I SAY HE GOT WORRYED! THIS MADE ME THINK WHAT KIND OF DOCTOR IS HE, MUST BE A CUT NO MATER WHAT, IF HE WAS FOR HIS PATIENTS HE WOULD HAVE STILL HAVE WANTED TO HELP ME, RIGHT. WELL I AM HERE TODAY TO SAY IT TOOK A VERY LONG TIME TO JUST HALF WAY HEALED, THIS HAPPENED AROUND 1988, WE ARE IN 2010. I LEARNED TO DO WHAT THE FIRST DOCTOR TOLD ME TO WATCH WHAT I DO AND I COULD LIVE WITHOUT THE OPERATION. I STILL HAVE TROUBLE, I CAN WORK FOR GOOD 20 MINUTES, BUT HAVE TO STOP, IF I WORK TO HARD, TROUBLE, LIGHT WORK LONGER. I DO HAVE TO TAKE LOTS OF BREAKS. MOST JOBS WILL NOT ALLOW THE BREAKS I NEED. BUT THIS WAS THE START OF SOMEONE ESE MESSING UP MY LIFE.

THE POINT IS, THE WEIGHT LOST PROGRAM I WAS ON CAUSED ME TO HAVE PROBLEMS, IN THIS CASE, TAKE MEDICINE TO LOWER BLOOD PRESURE THAT IT MADE COME UP, THIS WAS IN LATE 80S, I WENT FROM ABOUT 120-240 MG OF MEDS. BUT LATELY, I HAVE BEEN OFF SPICES, AND I HAD TO CHANGE MY DIET SOME, THE MEDICINE TROUBLES TORE UP MY STOMACH TO BAD, AND NOW I STILL TAKE MED. BUT ONLY SMALLER AMOUNT, ABOUT 5 MG OF BLOOD PRESURE MEDICINE. DOCTORS ALWAYS SAY LOSE WEIGHT YOUR BLOOD PRESSURE WILL COME DOWN, WELL THATS NOT ALLWAYS TRUE, AND I FOUND OUT THE HARD WAY. I DO EAT MORE THINGS THAT BOTHERED ME BEFORE, BUT I WANTED YOU TO SEE WHAT I WENT THROUGH.

THIS WAS THE START OF DIET PROGRAMS FOR ME THAT ARE MEANT TO HELP BUT DON'T, AT LEASE NOT THIS ONE, AND NOT IN THAT ERA OF TIME.

BY THE WAY I ESTIMATED THE MONEY I SPENT ON TAKING MEDICINE FOR THE BLOOD PRESSURE.

$50.00 FOR MEDS TIMES 12 MONTHS= $600.00 TIMES ABOUT 22 YEARS $13,200.00 THIS DOES NOT ENCLUDE DOCTOR VISIT OR GAS FOR GOING AND I COULD HAVE BOUGHT A BUICK I WANTED AT THAT TIME, COST FOR 1987 BUICK GRAND NATIONAL WAS ABOUT 12,000.00 I COULD NOT BUY THE CAR I WANTED BECAUSE I COULD NOT WORK FROM MY INJURY AT THAT TIME. BY THE WAY, THIS SAME CAR RESALE VALUE IS WAY UP THERE, I SAW ONE FOR AROUND 8,000.00 IN GOOD TO OK SHAPE. ONE WITH LESS THAT 10,000 MILES WAS ALMOST 100,000.00. REASON, LAST CAR BUICK MADE REAR WHEEL DRIVE AND HAD THE TURBO CHARGED V6 WITH THE INTERCOOL SYSTEM. YOU SAY WHATS THAT, ITS FAST. ONE BOOK SAID IT WOULD OUT RUN A CORVETTE BY FEW SECONDS, AND THE PEOPLE I KNOW THAT HAD ONE SAID WHEN THERE FOOT WASN'T IN THE INJECTION SYSTEM, IT WAS GOOD ON GAS.

NOW TROUBLE STARTS

TAKING DRUG 1 A STATIN DRUG—2 A ANTI INFLAMITORY DRUG AND 3 BLOOD PRESSURE DRUGS—WITHIN ONE WEEK OF STARTING I WAS FEELING WEARD AND MY EYES STARTED GIVING ME TROUBLE, BLURED VISION. MY EYE SIGHT HASN'T CHANGED HARDLY ANY IN OVER 10 YEARS UNTILL NOW, YES I CAN STILL SEE BUT DEVELOPED TROUBLE SEEING CLOSE UP, SOMETHING I NEVER HAD TROUBLE WITH, I TOOK UP ELECTRONICS AND WAS THE BEST AT SEEING SMALL PRINT OR CIRCUIT BOARDS, I SAW THINGS NO ONE COULD SEE, OR DIDN'T. IF YOU LOOK AT THE BACK OF YOUR WATCH YOU KNOW WHAT I MEAN. I COULD READ THAT AND SMALLER NO TROUBLE, NOW CAN'T SEE. THE EYE DR. RECOMMENDS BI FOCALS AT ABOUT 45-46 YEARS OLD.

JUST THINK OF THE MONEY FOR THE CHOLESTEROL MEDS, AND OTHERS, HOSPITAL ITS WAY UP THERE IN COST. JUST

ONE OF THE TEST THAT WAS DONE WAS OVER $1200.00, I WAS TOLD AND SOME WERE VERY PAINFULL TEST. ITS IN THIS BOOK, IF YOUR A MALE, IT HURTS!!!

THERE WAS A SITE I WENT TO ON THE NET THAT SAID 2 OF 3 PEOPLE THAT TOOK <u>STATIN DRUGS AND A BLOOD PRESSURE MEDICINE LIKE I HAD</u> AT HIGH DOSE'S WOULD HAVE A HEART ATTACK, IS THIS ME, THIS IS WHY I WROTE THIS BOOK, I'AM ALWAYS IN LINE OF A HEART ATTACK BECAUSE I TOOK MEDICINE THATS NOT SAFE? I WATCH FOR EVERY THING NOW, BUT STILL HAVE CHEST ACHES AND WONDER IS THIS IT. MY EKG'S ARE ALWAYS O.K., AT THE TIME I DO THEM AS OF NOW, I PRAY I'AM O.K. ALL THE TIME. DO I STILL HAVE THAT RIGHT TO PRAY? I KNOW I CAN NOT ACT ON WHAT I BELIEVE, AT LEAST NOT IN LOUISIANA, AND FEW OTHER STATES, THATS ANOTHER BOOK, THE LAWS YOU DON'T KNOW ABOUT TAKING YOUR RIGHTS AWAY.

THE LIST OF
SOME OF THE TESTS PERFORMED

CAT SCANS—FEW TIMES
X RAYS—MANY
HEART RECORDER—FEW TIMES
BLOOD WORK—LOTS
EYE EXAMINE 3 OR MORE
EAR & NOSE 2 OR MORE
BREATHING TEST 2
KIDNEY DOCTOR GO INTO BLADDER 3 TIMES
PAINFULL!!!!!!!
TEST FOR CK, LIVER, AND OTHERS
THROAT TEST 2 TIMES DOWN MOUTH
COLON MANY TIMES

COST? A LOT! STILL NEEDING MORE

P.A.D.

WHEN I WAS ON THE CHOLESTEROL MEDICINE/STATIN DRUGS I HAD HEAVINESS IN MY LEGS, HAD TROUBLE STANDING, IT WAS THE MEDICINE. WHY WHEN ON THIS MEDICINE I HAD P.A.D.? WHY I HAD LEG CRAMPS? I DON'T KNOW BUT I WOULD WAKE UP WITH LEGS STIFF LIKE BOARDS AT THE SAME TIME I WAS HAVING TROUBLE ONE DRUG COMPANY WAS ADVERTISING TO FIX THE SAME TROUBLE, THAT THEY CREATED! THIS IS WHAT I SAY, ALMOST EVERY TIME I HAD A NEW TROUBLE, THERE WAS A NEW PILL TO COUNTER REACT, IT WAS TIMED PERFECT. WHEN MY LEGS WERE STIFF, THERE WAS A PILL FOR THAT, THE ANXIETY ATTACKS THERE WERE MANY FOR THIS.

I SAW AN ADD ON TV WHERE <u>P.A.D. IS NOT REVERSABLE</u> ONCE YOU HAVE. I ALSO LOOKED UP ON THE INTERNET, ALL SITES I LOOKED AT SAY THE SAME, I HAD ALSO ASKED ONE OF MY DOCTORS. THE ADD ALSO SAYS P.A.D. COULD BE A SIGN OF TROUBLE FOR HEART ATTACK. IF THIS IS TRUE, THE WAY I SEE IT, THEN THESE MEDICINES CAN GIVE YOU A HEART ATTACK, JUST BECAUSE IT CAN CAUSE THIS PROBLEM. ITS THE ONLY LOGICAL ANSWER. I DO STILL HAVE WEAKNESS'S, BUT NOW I AM OFF ALL THE CHOLESTEROL MEDICINES, NOT NEAR AS BAD AS WHEN ON THE MEDICINES.

I COULD NOT BELIEVE AT THE SAME TIME THEY ARE PUSHING ONE DRUG, THERES ANOTHER ON TV TO FIX THE TROUBLE THE FIRST ONE GAVE. OF COURSE THEY DON'T SAY THAT. BUT IF YOU WERE TAKING THE DRUG AT THAT TIME AS I WAS, YOU WOULD KNOW WHAT I MEAN.

I DO STRESS—I BLAME THE CHOLESTEROL MEDICINE/STATIN DRUGS FOR EVERYTHING EVEN THOUGH SOME SIDE AFFECTS WERE FROM THE OTHER DRUGS. THE REASON, IS SIMPLE. IT'S THE REASON I HAD TO TAKE THE OTHER MEDICINES TO STOP SIDE AFFECTS, WHICH BY THE WAY BECAME A PERMANENT PART OF ME, AND THIS BOOK IS ABOUT TRYING TO COPE WITH THE TROUBLES I HAD AND STILL HAVE, AND LET THE PEOPLE KNOW THEY ARE NOT ALONE.

IF YOU LOOK UP P.A.D. YOU WILL SEE THE TROUBLES I HAD WERE THERE. YOU JUDGE, IF YOU GET OFF A DRUG AND THE PROBLEM GOES AWAY OR WEAKENS, ITS THE DRUG. IF THERE IS A ADVERTISEMENT THAT SAYS THIS CAN GIVE YOU THIS LIST OF TROUBLE, YOU WOULD SAY ITS THE MEDICINE, AND WHEN YOU GET OFF, WELL THE TROUBLE GOES AWAY OR WEAKENS A LOT. I THINK YOU GET THE PICTURE. BUT MY HORRORS ARE STILL THERE, WHY? WHAT DAMAGE DID THIS DO TO ME . . .

LET'S SAY IF P.A.D. IS CAUSED FROM THE MEDICINES I TOOK, WHICH STARTED WHEN I GOT ON THE MEDICINES. THEN LATER WHEN I GOT OFF THE MEDS THIS LEFT. THEN COMMON SENCE SAYS ITS THE MEDICINE. AND ALL THE AFFECTS THAT YOU HAVE FROM P.A.D. TV SAYS IF YOU HAVE P.A.D. THIS COULD BE A SIGN OF BLOCKED VEINS AND CAN LEAD TO STROKE. WELL THEN THE MEDICINE CAN CAUSE STROKES, RIGHT? ALL I KNOW IS AFTER ABOUT THE FIRST YEAR THE NURSE WAS HAVING TROUBLE FINDING VEINS. WHAT CAN I SAY. UNLESS YOU HAVE TAKEN THESE DRUGS AND HAVE HAD SOME OF THE TROUBLE. YOU KNOW WHAT I MEAN. IT'S BEEN A NIGHTMARE. IF YOU DON'T TAKE, ALL I CAN SAY IS LUCKY YOU, AND LUCKY YOU FOR NOT HAVING ANY TROUBLE WHAT SO EVER IF YOU DO TAKE, GO BUY A LOTTO TICKET YOUR LUCKY. I'VE TALKED TO OVER 1000 PEOPLE EASY THAT TOLD ME THERE GOING THROUGH THE SAME THING.

CAN'T TAKE THE HEAT!

ONE OF THE THINGS I FOUND OUT AFTER TAKING THE CHOLESTEROL MEDICINES WAS I CAN'T GO OUT AND DO NORMAL WORK. THIS KEPT ME FROM SOME JOBS THAT ARE IN HEAT RELATED AREAS. AT HOME I'D BE IN MY YARD WORKING OR JUST WALKING, I HAD A LOT OF LAND 8 ACRE'S TO TAKE CARE OF, I WOULD WORK FOR MAYBE 20 MINUTES SOMETIMES, AND THE HEAT WOULD JUST TAKE ALL MY ENERGY AWAY. I MEAN LIKE PLAYING A RECORD PLAYER AND UNPLUG IT, THE RECORD SLOWS DOWN FAST BUT YOU CAN HEAR THE SOUND MOST OF THE TIME BEFORE IT GOES AWAY, THATS' WHAT IT FELT LIKE. THERE WAS ONE TIME, I DIDN'T KNOW IF I WOULD MAKE IT BACK TO MY HOUSE, I WAS WORKING IN MY YARD IN THE BACK, AND STARTED FEELING WEAK, I STARTED TO WALK BACK TO MY HOUSE AND IT HIT ME BAD. WHEN I GOT WEAK, IT WAS SO FAST ITS UNREAL, I HAD ABOUT 150 TO 200 FEET TO WALK, I STARTED FAST AND THEN I STARTED WALKING SLOW, AND ONE POINT, WAS SURE I MAY HAVE TO CRAWL. I STOPPED FOR FEW SECONDS, RESTED, IT WAS HOT, I WANTED TO JUST LAY ON GRASS BUT WAS TO HOT, THE SUN WAS OUT, AND IT WAS IN THE FRY MODE. I FINDLY GOT THE ENERGY TO WALK, I MADE IT INSIDE AND LAIDED DOWN AND TOOK A NAP. I WAS ALWAYS TAKING NAPS THEY HELPED FOR A WHILE. I WOULD WAKE UP LIKE NOTHING HAPPENED, BUT IF I WOULD GO OUTSIDE, WELL WOULD START ALL OVER AGAIN, THE WEAKNESS DIDN'T TAKE LONG, NO MATTER WERE I WAS THE SAME THING WOULD HAPPEN. I HAD TO BE NEAR THE AIRCONDITIONER ALL THE TIME, OR IN THE CAR AND HAVE THE VENT BLOWING ON ME AT ALL TIMES. YOU WILL HEAR FROM MANY PEOPLE, THE SAME THING, THEY GET IN THE HEAT AND THEY ARE DRAINED! BUT DON'T KNOW WHY? I KNOW ONE PERSON WAS ON THE CHOLESTEROL MEDICINE

FOR ONLY 2 DAYS AND WAS IN THE HEAT, SHE JUST NEW SHE WAS DIEING. SHES OFF NOW AND BACK TO NORMAL, LUCKY HER, SO FAR.

WHEN SHE GOT SICK THIS HAPPENED JUNE 2010. DON'T REMEMBER WHICH DRUG SHE USED, SEEMS LIKE SHE SAID THE ONE THAT IS ADVERTISED TODAY AS FDA APROVED, YOU SEE IT ON TV. I TURN THE TV OFF SOMETIMES, THATS HOW UPSET THIS GETS ME. IT DON'T MATTER, <u>ALL STATIN DRUGS DONE THE SAME THING</u>. MESS YOUR LIFE AND HEALTH UP! ITS COST ME MY INHERITANCE, I HAD TO LIVE ON FOR A WHILE BECAUSE I WAS SO MESSED UP DIDN'T WANT TO DIE AT WORK, WAS HURTING SO MUCH AT TIMES, WOULD JUST STAY HOME. SOME TIME FOR DAYS, I KNOW OF ONE TIME A WEEK I WAS OFF. AND IT WASN'T FOR A VACATION! I WAS SURE I WAS DIEING. I STILL GET DRAINED BUT NOT NEAR AS BAD AS WHEN ON THE DRUG.

THIS IS THE WORSE MENTAL FEELING YOU CAN HAVE, YOU HAVE THE SKILLS TO DO ALMOST ANYTHING, AND CAN'T. I WOULD GET SO MAD AT MY BROTHER, HE'D TELL ME JUST GET A NEW JOB, BECAUSE I WAS LOSEING MONEY, YOU GOT GAS, DOCTOR VISITS, LOST OF WORK, MAINTAIN A CAR, HOUSE WORK, INSIDE AND OUT, I HELP MY SISTER AND MY MOTHER AND STEPDAD, WHO HAD JUST PASSED, MY DAD PASSED 2003. THE COST RUNS UP FAST! THERES TIMES JUST GOING TO THE STORE WAS A BIG DEAL. IF I STARTED HAVING A PANIC ATTACK, I WORRYED IF I WOULD MAKE IT OUT THE CHECKOUT LINE. THIS HAPPEN AT DEPT STORE, BROKE OUT IN A SWEAT AND WOULD GET WEAK, WAS SURE I WOULD PASS OUT SO I TOLD SOME ONE I DIDN'T FEEL GOOD. AND HAD A FRIEND IN THE STORE SO THEY COULD PAGE IF NEEDED. WHAT WOULD YOU DO NOT KNOWING? I WOULD MAKE MANY TRIPS SO I DIDN'T STAY OVER 10 MINUTES IN THE STORE, AND IF TO BUSY I WOULD JUST LEAVE AND COME BACK OR GO TO A QUICK STOP EVEN IF IT COST MORE. AT LEASE I WAS IN AND OUT QUICK!

I WORK IN THE AIRCONDITION MOST OF THE TIME SO I DON'T WANT TO LEAVE WHEN I KNOW HOW BAD THE HEAT MESS'S WITH ME. I DO GET OUT IN HEAT MORE NOW, BUT AT TIMES STILL BAD. I JUST CAN'T TAKE THE HEAT. I USED TO WORK ON A BOAT WHERE THE HEAT WAS HOT IN THE ENGINE ROOM, AND IT DIDN'T BOTHER ME. BUT WHEN I HAD TRYED TO WORK OFFSHORE AGAIN, I WAS WORRIED I WOULD HAVE TO STAY IN THERE FOR ANY LONG TIME FRAME, BUT DIDN'T AND IT WAS A GOOD AND EASY JOB. AND PAIDED $150.00 A DAY TO START, THE ENGINE ROOM WAS COOLER THAN SOME I HAD BEEN IN. I HAD A CHANCE TO MAKE MORE MONEY AT MANY COMPANYS, BUT TO MANY TROUBLES MEDICINE RELATED. ONE OTHER COMPANY I TESTED FOR, BUT FAILED THE ONE PART OF THE PHYSICAL TEST. PASSED EVERY THING BUT HOLDING ON TO A ROPE FOR 30 SECONDS. HELD ON FOR ABOUT 15-20 AND LET GO, THE GUY TOLD ME TO DO AGAIN, I COULD NOT DO TO SAVE MY LIVE. MY HANDS ARE STILL TO THIS DAY, WEAK!! CAN'T HOLD OR GRAB ANY THING TO HEAVY, WOULD DROP. I DROPPED A FILM REEL ON MY FOOT ALMOST BROKE MY FOOT, AND IT LEFT A MARK, WAS BLACK AND BLUE FOR A LONG TIME, THERE IS STILL A LITE MARK WHERE THIS FELL AND THE BONE IS RAISED. ALL BECAUSE OF CHOLESTEROL MEDICINE. EVEN THOUGH IT MAY BE THE OTHERS THAT HELPED GET LIKE THIS. THE CHOLESTEROL MEDICINE PUT ME ON THOSE BECAUSE OF ITS SIDE AFFECTS. AT LEAST THATS HOW I SEE IT. AND SO FAR I'VE BEEN RIGHT!!

I ALSO WANT TO SAY, ALMOST EVERYTHING YOU READ OR READ HAS HAPPENED ONE OR MORE TIMES. SOME THINGS I STILL HAVE TROUBLE WITH AS OF THIS WRITING. MOSTLY WEAKNESS AND BEING TIRED OR DRAINED ALL THE TIME. <u>DON'T THINK IT ONLY HAPPENED ONCE</u>. IF YOU TOOK THE CHOLESTEROL MEDICINE AND YOUR READING THIS NOW, YOUR NOW SAYING I KNOW WHAT YOU MEAN, THATS A FACT!!!!

NOTE: THE PICTURE OF MY FOOT WAS TAKEN LONG AFTER THE BLACK AND BLUE WAS GOING AWAY, THIS STAYED DARK BLACK & BLUE A LONG TIME AFTER DROPPING THE REEL ON IT.

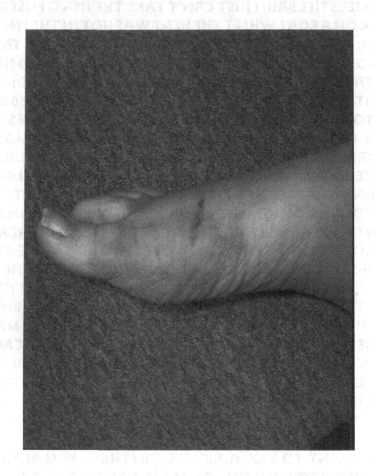

RETRAINED FOR NEW JOB AND CAN'T USE SKILLS

AFTER HURTING MY BACK I FOUND OUT I COULD RETRAIN FOR NEW JOBS, NOW CAN'T USE THAT TO MUCH. YES BEEN THERE DONE THAT, TOOK UP ELECTRONICS CAN FIX MOST NORMAL TROUBLES ON VCRS, BETA AND VHS.

NOW WE GOT DVDS NO VCRS TO WORRY ABOUT FIXING. I CAN FIX OLD RECORD PLAYERS, I RESTORE THE AMP OR CHANGER,

PUT IN A NEW CARTRAGE AS NEEDED, I COLLECT AND REPAIR THE OLD TUBE TYPE, WHEN THEY GET OLD THEY GET A HUM, EASY TO FIX, AND CHEAP, IN SOME CASES. BUT, BECAUSE OF ALL THE TROUBLES THE CHOLESTEROL MEDICINE GIVE ME, I HAVE MUCH TROUBLE BREATHING I DON'T HARDLY TOUCH. ONLY MY OWN AND ONLY EVERY NOW AND THEN. THIS STUFF MESSED MY LIFE UP IN SO MANY WAYS ITS UNREAL. I WAS WEAK ALL DAY TODAY AND EVEN NOW WHILE TYPING. THE MEDS MESSED UP MY EYES, I WAS ABLE TO SEE CIRCUIT BOARDS, I CAN'T SEE CLOSE UP ANY MORE NOT LIKE I USED TO. HERES A LIST OF JOBS I CAN DO BUT CAN'T DO, ARE CAN'T DO WITH OUT SOME KIND OF TROUBLE. I USED TO DO ALL MY OWN CAR REPAIRS, I CAN FIX ALMOST ANYTHING ON MY CARS, ALL BUT THE TRANSMISSION, WILL NOT TOUCH THIS, WILL CHANGE SEALS ON THE ENDS, I STILL DO MY OWN AC WORK, LEARNED FROM THE BEST, AND ON HAND TRAINING. I NEVER HAD TROUBLE WITH ANY JOBS I DONE, MY 1983 BUICK AC HAS BEEN ON SINCE ABOUT 1992-3 AND STILL GETS VERY COLD, ABOUT 33 DEGREES AT VENT, HAVE PICTURE. THIS IS AFTER ABOUT 30 MIN. OF DRIVING.

WORK ON BOATS (TRYED AGAIN)LOSTED JOB BECAUSE OF MEDS. ELECTRONICS (TRYED AGAIN) SMELLS AFFECT BREATHING PROJECTIONIST DOING NOW BUT I 'AM IN PAIN EVERY DAY!!! UP AND DOWN STAIRS PAINT CAR & LITE BODY WORK—GET SICK-LITE HEADED WORK ON CAR AC—CAN'T TAKE THE HEAT REBUILD ENGINES—WEAK ALL THE TIME, AND STILL HAVE BACK TROUBLE DRIVE TRUCKS—(LONG AS I DON'T LIFT, YEA RIGHT) WITH WEAK SPELLS WOULD WORRY ABOUT BEING ON TRIPS, COULD DJ AGAIN, NO PAY ALL THE GOOD PAYING JOBS I WOULD HAVE SO MUCH TROUBLE TRYING. AND MOST OWNERS DON'T LIKE THAT IDEA OF SOMEONE TAKING OFF ALL THE TIME FOR DOCTOR VISITS, OR PANIC ATTACKS I THINK THEY WOULD WORRY IF I WOULD TELL.

I MUST NOTE THE RETRAINING WAS AFTER MY FIRST BOUT WITH TROUBLES.

WHAT 2 DOCTORS TOLD ME

I ALSO MET TWO DOCTORS AT TWO DIFFERENT TIMES. THIS IS WHEN I WAS HAVING THE VERY BAD TROUBLES WITH THE CHOLESTEROL MEDICINE I WAS ON LAST. WHEN THEY FOUND OUT WHAT I WAS ON AND AFTER TALKING TO THEM, THEY BOTH HAD TOLD ME THEY HAD BOTH BEEN ON THE MEDICINE AT ONE TIME AND THIS WAS WHY I WAS HAVING TROUBLE. ONE DOCTOR TOLD ME TO GET OFF, "IT WILL KILL ME" IF I KEEP ON THIS MEDICINE. I THINK I HAVE THE PAPER WHERE IT WAS PUT ON MY MEDICAL RECORDS. BOTH DOCTORS HAD THE SAME TROUBLES THAT I HAD SO WHEN THEY GOT TO SEE SOMEONE LIKE ME, THEY SAW THE SIDE AFFECTS I WAS HAVING AND THE MEDICINES I WAS ON WAS FROM ME TAKING THE CHOLESTEROL MEDICINE. AGAIN THEY HAD BOTH TOLD ME THEY TOOK THE MEDICINE AND HAD TROUBLE. THEY BOTH TOLD ME THEY WOULD NOT PRESCRIBE ANY OF THIS MEDICINE UNLESS A DIET DIDN'T WORK, AND THEN WOULD HAVE TO THINK ON THIS FIRST. THESE DOCTORS DON'T WANT YOU TO JUST EAT WHAT YOU WANT AND TAKE A PILL TO CORRECT. THATS NOT GOOD FOR YOUR HEALTH. I SURE THANK THEM NOW FOR HELPING ME REALIZE IT WAS THE MEDS & THANK THEM FOR NOT HURTING ANYONE BY GIVING PRESCRIPTIONS OUT FOR THIS. I WAS TOLD TO CHANGE MY DIET AND EAT FOODS YOU KNOW ARE LOW IN CHOLESTEROL, OR LOOK UP ON THE NET, OR GET BOOKS.

I WANT TO SAY AGAIN, THESE TWO DOCTORS TOLD ME THIS IN PERSON, SOMEWHERE IN THE BOOK I TALK ABOUT MY UNCLES DOCTOR SAID THIS WAS BAD STUFF AND TOOK HIM OFF BUT WAS TO LATE, MY UNCLE HAD TOLD ME WHEN HE FOUND OUT HE HAD THE CANCER THE DOCTOR SAID GET OFF ALL MEDICINES. IF YOU LOOK ON THE INTERNET FOR ANY OF

THE CHOLESTEROL MEDS, (ANY ONE) THERES A GOOD CHANCE YOU'LL SEE MORE BAD HORROR STORYS, I ONLY LOOKED AT A FEW. I SEE AND HEAR OF TROUBLES ALMOST EVERY DAY, YESTERDAY, OCTOBER 6, 2010, I HEARD A 24 YEAR OLD MAN WAS HAVING TROUBLE, HIS MOTHER WAS TELLING ME HE HAD TROUBLE AFTER BEING PUT ON CHOLESTEROL MEDICATION, AFTER SHE WAS FINISHED, I TOLD HER MINE. I ALSO TOLD HER WHAT I WAS DOING, TELLING PEOPLE ABOUT MY TROUBLES AND OTHERS LIKE HIM, I TOLD HER, HES NOT ALONE WITH HIS TROUBLES.

BURNING EYES

THERE WERE TIMES WHEN MY EYES FELT LIKE THEY WERE ON FIRE ON THE INSIDE OUT. THE BEST WAY TO EXPLAIN IS A FEVER INSIDE THE EYE, AND HOT!

NOBODY EVER TOLD ME WHY OR DONE ANY TEST ON ME FOR THAT. AFTER GETTING OFF THE MEDICINES THIS BAD BURNING SEEM TO HAVE LEFT. I STILL HAVE ONCE AND A WHILE, BUT NOT THE SAME AS BEFORE. ONE DOCTOR SAID MAY BE THE CHEMICALS IN THE AIR, ALL I KNOW IS ONCE OFF ALL THE MEDICATIONS SEEM TO GO AWAY, AT LEAST THE BAD PART OF BURNING, I HAVENT HAD IN A LONG TIME AS OF THIS WRITING. I DID SEEM TO NOTICE EACH TIME I HAD THE BURNING IT WAS AFTER NOT CRAPPING FOR A LONG PERIOD, WHICH I DO STILL HAVE TROUBLE WITH EVEN TODAY, THERE ARE TIMES ITS NOT SO BAD BUT OTHER TIMES FEELS LIKE OLD TIMES, YOU SEEM TO GO FOR 2-3 DAYS OR MORE BEFORE YOU RELIZED YOU ARE NOT FEELING RIGHT AND YOU HAVE NOT POOPED. THEY DO GO TOGETHER AND THESE DRUGS I WAS ON SHURE MESSED UP MY SYSTEM, EVEN TO THIS DAY, JAN. 31, 2012, IAM GOING TO THE DOCTOR TODAY IF I CAN FOR JUST THIS. STOMACH WAS HURTING LAST NIGHT AND PICKING ON MY LEFT AREA AND I HAVNT HARDLY GONE IN DAYS.

HAVE HAD A WEARD EAR ACHE AND EYE ACHES TOGETHER LEFT SIDE OF HEAD, ITS LIKE A EAR ACHE BUT FURTHER IN THE HEAD AND EYE WAS SAME, FURTHER IN THAN NORMAL, ALMOST THE CENTER OF MY HEAD. (SEE THE DRAWING)

MY STEP DAD HAD THIS ALSO, HE TOLD ME THEY CUT SOME NERVE TO HELP, I TOLD HIM HOW MINE FELT AND HE SAID

THAT WAS EXACTLY LIKE HIS PROBLEM. AFTER HE WAS CUT ON HE SAID HE HAD VISION TROUBLE. I THINK HIS TROUBLE WAS LIKE MINE, FROM THE CHOLESTEROL MEDICINES. HE LATER GOT OFF WHEN I GOT OFF, HE SAW I WAS FEELING BETTER OFF THE MEDICINE, SO HE GOT OFF AND NEVER TOOK AGAIN. IT WAS SOME TIME LATER MY MOTHER FOLLOWED. I THINK IT WAS OVER 1 YEAR LATER BEFORE HE HAD TO GO TO THE HOSPITAL & WHEN HE DID GO, IT WAS TO LEARN HE HAD CANCER.

NOTE: see pictures

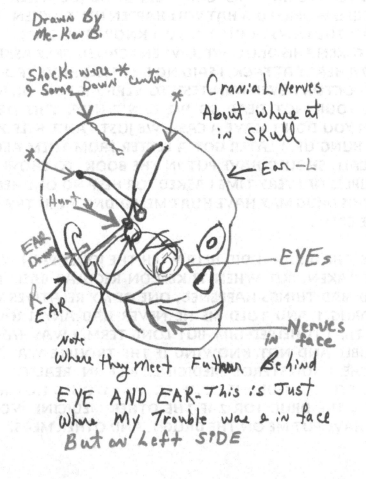

Drawn By
Me - Kew B.

Shocks were * center
& Some Down

Cranial Nerves
About where at
in Skull

← Ear -L

EAR
Down

Hurt

R
EAR

EYEs

Note

Nerves
in face

Where they meet Futher Behind
EYE AND EAR - This is Just
Where My Trouble was & in face
But on Left SIDE

DRUG-1 & 2

WHEN ON THE DRUG 1&2 ANTI IMFLAMITORY DRUG IT FELT LIKE MY SKIN ON MY HEAD WAS BEING PULLED OVER MY HEAD. BLOOD PULSING IN MY NECK & HURT. MUSCLE ACHES,& HORROR OF NOT KNOWING OF A HEART ATTACK, REMEMBER TAKING THE CHOLESTEROL MEDICINE WAS TO STOP OR PREVENT ONE. WITH ALL MY TROUBLE IT WAS HARD TO LIVE LIKE THIS, CAN'T GET GOOD JOB WHEN THIS WEAK!! & WORRYED WHAT WILL HAPPEN NEXT. WHEN I HAD CALLED THE LAWYER ON TV, YOU KNOW THE ONES, HAVE YOU TAKEN THIS DRUG, WELL WHEN I CALLED THEY ASKED IF I HAD A HEART ATTACK, I SAID NO BUT STILL HAVE TROUBLE AND DOCTOR NEVER RUN TEST TO VERIFY IF I DID OR NOT. WELL YOUR NOT DEAD SO WE CAN'T HELP. THIS DON'T MEAN YOU DON'T HAVE A CASE, WE JUST CAN'T HELP YOU, AND HUNG UP. I LATER GOT A LETTER FROM THEM ABOUT THE CALL, SHOULD HAVE PUT IN THE BOOK, TO SHOW THE TROUBLES OF EVERY TIME I ASKED FOR HELP NO ONE HELPED ME, THIS DRUG MAY HAVE HURT ME. I DIDN'T EVEN TRY ANY MORE CALLS.

NOTE: THE DRUG—1 DID HELP WITH THE JOINT PAIN WHEN FIRST TAKEN, BUT WHEN TAKEN ON REGULAR BASIS NOT GOOD, BAD THINGS HAPPENED. ONE OF MY RELATIVES WAS ON DRUG 1 AND TOLD ME HE NEVER HAD ANY TROUBLE AND THAT IT HELPED HIM. BUT LONG TERM, I WAS HAVING TROUBLE AND NOT KNOWING IF THE TROUBLE WAS THIS OR THE CHOLESTEROL MEDICINE. BUT IN REALITY, THE CHOLESTEROL MEDICINE IS. AFTER ALL I WOULD NOT HAVE TAKEN THE DRUG 1OR 2 IF THE OTHER MEDICINE WOULD NOT HAVE PUT ME ON THE DRUG 1, AND OTHER MEDS.

HEART ATTACK?

RUSHED MYSELF TO THE HOSPITAL MANY TIMES, THIS ONE TIME I WENT TO LOCAL CITY HOSPITAL. THIS WAS AROUND THE TIME I WAS ON DRUG 1 AN INFLAMITORY DRUG. I WAS ON THE WAY TO WORK AND PULLED OVER ACROSS THE STREET FROM WORK AND CALLED MY RELIEF, I ASKED HIM TO GO IN TO WORK, HE SAID YES SO I WENT ON TO THE HOSPITAL. I HAD BROKEOUT IN A SWEAT, AND STARTED HAVING TROUBLE BREATHING, THINK THIS MAY HAVE BEEN MY FIRST ANXIETY ATTACK, NOT SURE.

WAS ALSO HAVING MY HEAD FEEL LIKE THE SKIN TIGHTED OVER UP ON, AND THE BLOOD WAS PULSEING IN MY NECK SO HARD I WAS SURE SOMEONE NEAR BY WOULD FEEL ALSO. ANYWAY AFTER ALL TEST WHERE DONE THERE, THEY SENT ME HOME BUT NEVER TOLD ME WHAT IT MAY HAVE BEEN AT THIS TIME. (IT WAS AROUND THIS TIME ONE DOCTOR SAID I MAY HAVE HAD AN ANXIETY ATTACK, I DON'T THINK SO BUT WAS LATER PUT ON DRUG—3 ANXIETY DRUG, I WAS ON AT LEAST 3 PILLS AT THIS TIME, BUT NEW IT HAD TO BE THE IS DRUG 1. LATER AFTER HAVING MORE TROUBLE AND NO ONE TELLING ME WHAT WAS WRONG, I TOOK MY SELF OFF THE DRUG, I STOPPED HAVING MOST OF MY TROUBLE. IT WAS ABOUT 2 WEEKS LATER I SAW ONE OF THOSE FAMOUS ADDS, HAVE YOU TAKEN THIS DRUG, CALL NOW. I DIDN'T LIKE WHAT THEY TOLD ME, AND DIDN'T HELP. I NOW KNOW THAT MANY OF THE DRUGS I WAS ON HAD SOME OF THE SAME SIDE AFFECTS, SO WHICH ONE WAS CAUSEING THE WORSE? MAYBE IT WAS DOUBLED, DON'T KNOW JUST KNOW NOW IT WAS ALL THE DRUGS AND I COULD HAVE DIED THEN OR EVEN NOW, DON'T KNOW WHATS LERKING FROM LONG TERM USE OF THESE DRUGS. LIKE I'VE SAID IN THIS BOOK, EVERY DAY A NEW ADVENTURE. I DO WANT TO NOTE WAS ON BOTH MEDICINES IN THE TITLE AND FOR SAME USE, I HAVE DRUG 1 DOWN BECAUSE IT WAS THE FIRST AND TOOK THE LONGEST I BELIEVE.

THE COURT ADVENTURE

BACK WHEN I WAS HAVING BAD ANXIETY ATTACKS, AND OFTEN, I WAS SUMMONED TO GO TO COURT, NEVER BEEN IN COURT FOR A TRAIL, AND THIS ONE WAS A BOAT TRAIL WHERE SOMEONE WAS HURT. I HAD BEEN IN THAT PLACE ALREADY AND WANTED TO GO, I'AM A FAIR PERSON AND WOULD RESPECT THE COMPANYS VIEWS, BUT SURE WOULD HAVE LIKE TO STAY. NOW, NOT KNOWING WHEN I WOULD HAVE A PANIC ATTACK I HAD TO TELL THE JUDGE I HAVE ANXIETY ATTACKS WHERE I WOULD HAVE TROUBLE BREATHING AND IT WOULD FEEL LIKE I WAS HAVING A HEART ATTACK. THE JUDGE LOOKED AT ME AND SAID, YOUR FREE TO GO, HE SMILED AND SAID THERE'S GONNA BE SOME HIGH ANXIETY FLYING IN THIS COURT ROOM WHEN WE START. I WAS ALL WORRED ABOUT THAT, SOMETHING AS SIMPLE AS JUST SITTING IN A COURT ROOM KNOWING ONCE I'AM IN THERE, I'AM LOCKED IN. WHEN YOU HAVE THESE ATTACKS THATS THE LAST THING YOU NEED IS THE FEELING OF NO FREEDOM. I WOULD PUT WATER ON MY FACE SOMETIMES WHEN I WAS IN A PLACE OF CONFINDMENT. SOMETIMES IT HELPED TO CLOSE MY EYES AND FIND THAT HAPPY PLACE LIKE I HEARD IN SOME MOVIE, OR THINK OF A RELAXING SONG.

ELEVATOR ADVENTURE

ONE TIME I WAS ON A ELEVATOR, AND IT STOPPED, THE MAN WAS LEAVING THE BUILDING AS I WAS COMING IN, I BROKE DOWN AND WAS SWEATING IN A PLACE I WOULD BE COLD. ITS THE IDEA OF KNOWING YOU CAN'T MOVE LIKE YOU WANT THAT BRINGS THESE ATTACKS. THE GUY WAS STOPPED IN TIME BEFORE LEAVING AND GOT US MOVING. I WALKED DOWN THE STAIRS WHEN I LEFT.

THE DENTIST TRIP

I WAS SEEING THE DENTIST FOR SOME TIME TO FIX MY TEETH PUT CROWNS ON AND OTHER THINGS MESSED UP FROM A WRECK BACK IN THE 70S LOST FRONT TWO TEETH. WHILE IN THE CHAIR I STARTED HAVING A PANIC ATTACK WHILE HE WAS WORKING ON ME. THE DOCTOR DIDN'T KNOW WHAT WAS GOING ON, I DIDN'T AT THE TIME EITHER. I KNEW MY BLOOD SUGAR MADE ME NOT FEEL RIGHT SO HE SENT SOMEONE TO GET ORANGE JUICE. I FELT LIKE I WAS ON PINS AND NEEDLES WORRING ABOUT IF I WOULD PANIC, WAS HAVING TROUBLE BREATHING. BUT HE WASN'T FINISHED YET. I GOT THAT DONE AND LATER I READ I MAY BE MORE SENSITIVE TO DRUGS, SO NEXT TIME I SAW HIM I TOLD HIM. I LATER WHEN BACK TO GET A TOOTH PULLED BECAUSE I LET IT GO TO FAR, I WAS SCARED TO GO BACK AND HAVE THE SAME THING HAPPEN. I WAS OFF THE DRUGS BY THIS TIME BUT STILL WOULD HAVE HIGH ANXIETY AND WAS AT THE EDGE OF MY SEAT THE HOLD TIME. I NEED TO GO NOW AND SEE HIM BUT WORRED, NEED TO FINISH MY TEETH, MAYBE HE CAN PUT ME TO SLEEP? I DON'T KNOW ANY MORE. I DID SEE A SIGN IN HIS OFFICE LATER ABOUT PEOPLE ON CERTAIN DRUGS TO LET HIM KNOW.
I SHOULD GET HIS THOUGHTS ON WHAT HAPPENED BUT DON'T WANT TO TAKE UP HIS TIME, I AM SURE HE COULD TELL YOU HE WAS WORRIED, AFTER ALL HE SENT A WORKER TO GET ORANGE JUICE FOR ME. HE COULD HAVE SAD JUST LEAVE, GO SEE THE YOUR DOCTOR. DR WISE IS A GREAT DENTIST, AND CAN WORK WONDERS.

SUGAR LEVELS DROPED

WHEN I WAS ON THE CHOLESTEROL MEDICINE, ONE DAY I STARTED FEELING NOT RIGHT, LIKE MY DAD TOLD ME HE FEELS LIKE WHEN HIS SUGAR WAS TO LOW, WAS NEAR HIS HOUSE, SO STOPPED IN AND CHECKED. SURE WAS LOW. I GOT SOMETHING SWEET, AFTER FEW MINUTES I FELT GOOD AGAIN.

THIS WENT ON FOR SOME TIME, WHERE I WAS ALWAYS CHECKING AFTER THAT. FEW TIMES TOLD DOCTOR WHAT HAPPENED. THE DOCTOR DONE TEST AND SAID I WAS NOT DIEBETIC. BUT SAID I SHOULD DO WHAT I HAD BEEN DOING, CHECKING MY SUGAR ON REGULAR BASIS.

ONE DAY WAS FEELING WORSE THAN I EVER BEEN JUST REALY WOSZY. WASN'T NEAR A BLOOD CHECKER SO I JUST ATE A HALF CUP OF SUGAR AND DRANK SOME ORANGE JUICE IF I REMEMBER RIGHT, AFTER FEELING A LOT BETTER I GOT IN MY CAR AND DROVE TO MY MOTHERS HOUSE WE CHECKED MY SUGAR, IT WAS AROUND 50 OR 55 I CHECKED FEW MORE TIMES, STILL LOW BUT WAS COMING UP AND I WAS FEELING BETTER, THIS IS ABOUT 1/2 HOUR AFTER I ATE THE SUGAR AND DRANK THE ORANGE JUICE. MUST HAVE REALY BEEN LOW.

FROM THIS TIME ON I WATCHED MORE OF EVERY THING I ATE, DRANK, OR DONE. MY WHOLE LIFE WAS UPSIDE DOWN, DIDN'T KNOW WHAT WAS GOING TO HAPPEN NEXT. I HAD BEEN LOOKING FOR A BETTER JOB AND EVERY TIME THIS HAPPENED OR SOMETHING ESE, I WOULD HOPE I WOULDN'T GET HIRED BECAUSE DIDN'T KNOW WHAT WOULD HAPPEN ON THE JOB. I COULD PASS OUT AND HURT SOMEONE, OR

29

JUST DRIVING TO WORK I WAS ALWAYS THINKING IF I FELT LIKE PASSING OUT PULL OVER FAST AND CUT ENGINE, IF I COULD'NT BRAKE THE CAR WOULD STILL STOP.

I STILL CHECK TODAY, BUT VERY SELDOM HAVE ANY TROUBLE NOW I AM OFF THE CHOLESTEROL MEDICINE. IT TOOK A LONG TIME JUST TO GET WHERE I AM NOW, STILL MESSED UP BUT NOT AS BAD. JUST LOTS OF PAIN IN JOINTS RIGHT AND LEFT SIDE AND STILL HAVE FEW WEAK SPELLS.

THE LAST TIME I HAD SUGAR PROBLEMS WAS AGAIN, MEDICINE. I HAD GOTTIN CONSIPATED AND WAS GIVEN SOMETHING TO HELP AND IT TASTED GOOD, LIKE THAT SYRUP IN THE CAN. AFTER A FEW MINNUTES FELT WEARD, CHECKED SUGAR WAS ABOUT 280 AND LATER 300 THE HOSPITAL TOLD ME THIS WAS NORMAL FOR THE MEDICINE I TOOK AND IT WOULD COME DOWN. AFTER FINDLY GOING TO SLEEP I WOKE UP OK, AT LEAST FOR A WHILE.

AT ONE TIME I WAS SURE I HAD DEVELOPED HYPOGLYCEMIA? JUST WAITING TO DIE, NOT KNOWING WHEN THIS WOULD HAPPEN AGAIN, AND WOULD I BE NEAR SUGAR, I WANTED TO WORK OFFSHORE AGAIN AND THIS IS WHY I KEEP PUTING OFF LOOKING FOR A JOB WHERE I WOULD BE AWAY FROM A DOCTOR TO FAR AWAY. I COULD BE ON A BOAT, OR RIG WITH THE ANXIETY I WAS HAVING IT WAS JUST HORRABLE JUST THINKING OF IT. THE NOT KNOWING WHAT OR WHEN AN ATTACK WOULD COME. THERE ARE SOME STUDYS THAT THINK THERES A RELATION TO DIABETIS, WHEN ON CHOLESTROL MEDICINE. I SAY YES I AM NOT A DOCTOR BUT COMMON SENCE TELLS ME FROM WHAT I'VE SEEN AND HEARD MANY PEOPLE ON THIS DRUG SAY LATER THEY SEEM TO BECOME A DIEBETIC. THESE DRUGS MESSED MY LEVELS OF SUGAR, AND I CRAVED SALT. DON'T KNOW WHY, SEEM TO FEEL BETTER AFTER TAKING JUST A PINCH. I DO KNOW SOME MEDICINES REMOVE CERTAIN VITAMINS FROM YOUR BODY, WHEN ON THE LIQUID DIET I HAD TO TAKE POTASSIUM PILLS. ME, I ATE BANNANAS ALSO.

WHAT IS HYPOGLYCEMIA? THIS IS A CONDITION THAT OCCURS WHEN YOUR BLOOD SUGAR IS TO LOW
BLOOD SUGAR (GLUCOSE) LEVELS
SOME SYMPTOMS I HAD: COLD SWEATS—CONFUSION—GENERAL DISCOMFORT, UNEASINESS, OR ILL FEELING—TREMBLING—RAPID HEART RATE—NERVOUSNESS—HUNGER—HEADACHE

OTHER SYMPTOMS THAT MAY BE ASSOCIATED WITH THIS DISEASE:

DECREASED ALERTNESS—DIZZINESS—FAINTING—MUSCLE PAIN—POUNDING HEARTBEAT

I HAD SOME OF THESE HAPPEN TO ME WHILE I WAS ON THE MEDS. YOU CAN LOOK UP MORE OF THIS ON THE INTERNET. EVERY THING I'AM WRITING ABOUT THAT HAPPENED TO ME CAN BE SEEN ON THE NET. THERES SITES THAT TALK ABOUT DIFFERENT DRUGS, I THOUGHT I WAS GOING NUTS WHEN SOME OF THESE WEARD THINGS HAPPENED TO ME, NEVER KNEW WHAT WAS GOING ON UNTILL STARTED TALKING TO OTHER PEOPLE WITH SAME TROUBLES, THEY TO WOULD SAY <u>THE DOCTOR DIDN'T BELIEVE OR DIDN'T THINK IT WAS THE MEDICINE. YOU ARE NOT ALONE!!!!</u>

STIFF LEGS

I WOULD WAKE UP WITH MY LEGS STIFF LIKE A BOARD, AND MY MUSCLES WOULD BE HURTING

REAL BAD ONCE AWAKE, THEY RELAXED BUT HURT FOR A WHILE. AFTER THIS HAPPENED FOR A FEW MONTHS THATS WHEN I NOTICE MY JOINTS IN THE KNEE WERE HURTING MORE AND MORE AND THE PAIN WAS NOT LEAVING ME AS OFTEN. EACH TIME I WOKE UP IT WAS WORST. (THIS WHILE I WAS ON ALL THE MEDS) I HATED TO GO TO SLEEP KNOWING THE PAIN WOULD WAKE UP. THIS LATER GREW INTO PAIN SO BAD AT TIMES I WOULD ALMOST CRY. I TOOK OFF OF WORK OFTEN, BECAUSE WHERE I WORK I HAVE TO WALK UP AND DOWN THE STAIRS AT MINIMUM, 2 TIMES A DAY, BUT THIS ISN'T THAT OFTEN, I ALSO HAVE TO WALK ABOUT 300' FT. ACROSS THE BUILDING, TO START THE PROJECTORS AND BACK, THEN AT LEAST TWICE A HOUR WALK AND CHECK THE MOVIE SCREEN. IF I CHECK THE SOUND LEVEL I HAVE TO GO BACK DOWN STAIRS TO EACH MOVIE SCREEN, TO MAKE SURE SOUND IS JUST RIGHT. WEEKENDS IF I COLLECT TICKETS, EVERY FEATURE, UP AND DOWN STAIRS, I AM IN PAIN ALL DAY. I CAN'T TAKE PAIN MEDICINE, IF I DO, I WANT TO SLEEP. I WORK FOR MY RELATIVES, IF THIS WAS SOMEONE ESE. I'D BE GONE. I'AM ALLOWED TO TAKE SOME MEDS OR PART WHEN NEEDED, THEY TRUST MY JUDGEMENT BUT DON'T WANT ME PASSED OUT. I MAY TAKE UP TO 1/2 PAIN PILL TO TAKE OUT MOST OF THE PAIN. ANY MORE, I HAVE TO TAKE ANOTHER DAY OFF.

I TOOK OFF WORK SO MANY TIMES I LOST TRACK OF. AND THIS PAIN COST ME MONEY FROM WORK, AND MY HEALTH, ALSO FUEL TO GO TO DOCTORS THAT WOULDN'T HELP ALL THE

TIME. I WANTED TO KNOW WHY FOR SURE I WAS HURTING. FINELY I GOT A X-RAY AT ONE POINT. DIDN'T SEE ANYTHING. BUT NO KAT SCAN—JUST TOOK ANOTHER X-RAY FOR A KNEE I HURT FROM A WEAK SPELL, BUT THE DOCTOR HASN'T SAID ANY THING AT THE TIME OF THIS WRITING. GETING BACK TO STIFF LEGS, AS I SAID THEY ALL SEEM TO OVER LAP IN PAIN AND TROUBLE FROM ONE MED TO NEXT. AFTER I HAD GOT OFF OF THE MEDICINE I WAS ON AT THE TIME THE PAIN SEEM TO EASE UP, BUT HAD NEVER LEFT!!! I NOW HAVE PERMANENT JOINT PAINTS, FACT! THE LEVELS OF PAIN COME AND GO, FROM #5 MEDIUM TO 10+ PAIN, I JUST WANT TO TAKE A PAIN PILL AND SLEEP IT OFF SOMETIMES. I ALSO WANT TO SAY, AT THE TIME THIS WAS HAPPENING TO ME A NEW PILL COME OUT, DON'T KNOW THE NAME BUT WHAT YOU THINK IT WAS FOR, STIFF LEGS, EVERY TIME I SEEM TO HAVE TROUBLE WHILE ON THIS MEDICINE, AS TIME WHEN ON I HAD NEW TROUBLE, THERE WAS A NEW PILL. THEY KNEW WHAT THIS MEDICINE WAS DOING THATS WHY THE NEWER MEDICINE WAS TO CORRECT THE TROUBLE OF THE SECOND PILL OR THE THIRD. AT TIMES YOU FORGET WHICH PILL WAS TO HELP WHAT PAIN FROM THE OTHER PILL. CONFUSED? I THINK YOU GET THE POINT. OH YEA, CONFUSION WAS ANOTHER SIDE AFFECT OF ONE OF THE MEDS I WAS ON. I JUST KNOW MY FAITH IN GOD IS WHAT KEPT ME AS STABLE AS I COULD GET. WHEN I TELL SOME PEOPLE THESE THINGS, THEY SAY THEY WOULD GO NUTS.

BLADDER INFECTIONS

THE WHOLE TIME I WAS ON THE CHOLESTEROL MEDS, I SEEM TO KEEP HAVING BLADDER INFECTIONS OR IRITATIONS. EVEN DRINKING TEA WOULD SET OFF, IF I TRY TO DRINK A LOT OF TEA WAS WORSE. I STILL AM VERY SINSITIVE TO THINGS I DRINK. I RECENTLY HAD A BACTERA INFECTION NOT LONG AFTER DRINKIN WATER THAT WAS NOT SAFE, MY TOWN DRINKING WATER. I GET LETTERS WHEN NOT TO DRINK BUT ONLY AFTER SHOULD NOT BE DRINKING. AT LEAST, SEEMS THAT WAY. WHEN ON THE MEDICINES I SEEM TO HAVE BLADDER TROUBLE OFTEN. EVEN WHEN I DRANK BOTTLE WATER. I DON'T KNOW WHATS WRONG BUT I SEEM TO BE MORE PRONE TO GETTING THESE NOW. I ALSO WONDER ABOUT THE BOTTLE WATER THAT I DRINK TO SOMETIMES HAS A BITTER TASTE. TRYED TO CONTACT THE COMPANY BUT THEY NEVER ME BACK. I EVEN FOUND A PIECE OF RUBBER IN MY BOTTLE ONE TIME, LITE GREEN, SURE WAS SOME KIND OF A SEAL BUT LOOK LIKE THERE WOULD BE SOME KIND OF SCREEN TO FILTER OUT.

I HAD A LOTS OF TEST DONE WHICH ARE IN THIS BOOK. ONE TIME A DOCTOR TOLD ME HE SAW A SHADOW ON MY KIDNEY. THERE WHERE TEST DONE MONTHS LATER AGAIN, STILL HAD BLOOD IN MY URINE, BUT DIDN'T SEE THE SAME SHADOW HE TALKED ABOUT, THIS WAS AGAIN AFTER I HAD GOT OFF SOME OF MY MEDICINES. WHEN I WOULD GET OFF ONE FOR A WHILE, SEEM TO FEEL BETTER AND GET BETTER, BUT DOCTOR WOULD TELL ME HE HAD ANOTHER DRUG TO TAKE FOR CHOLESTEROL. AT NO TIME I REMEMBER ANYONE SAYING JUST STAY AWAY FROM CERTAIN FOODS. LATER WHEN I GOT OFF OF ALL THE CHOLESTEROL MEDICINES, I WENT TO 2% MILK AND MORE BRAND FLAKES, NO CHEESE, I ALSO GOT OFF OF SPICES, THIS

ALONE MADE A BIG DIFFERENCE. BLOOD PRESSURE HAD COME DOWN AND HAD TO GET OFF ONE OF MY BLOOD PRESSURE MEDICINES. I DID NOTICE SOME FOODS AND DRINKS WOULD NOT MAKE ME FEEL RIGHT. I STARTED WITH ORGANIC MILK. I SEEM TO FEEL BETTER MORE OFTEN. FEW TIMES WENT BACK TO THE OTHER MILK NOTICE MORE HEADACHES AND JUST DIDN'T FEEL RIGHT AT TIMES. MY MOTHER NOTICED ALSO, SO NOW WE ONLY GET THE ORGANIC MILK WHEN EVER WE CAN. GOT AWAY FROM THE BLADDER BUT AGAIN I ASK, IS IT THE MEDICINES PLUS EVERY THING WE EAT, ALL THE THINGS THEY PUT IN YOUR CANDY, FOOD, DRINKS, YOU MAY NOTICE SOME OF THE SAME THINGS. WHEN YOUR FEELING GOOD AND YOU EAT OR DRINK SOMETHING MAKE A MENTAL NOTE. IF HAPPENS AGAIN FIND OUT WHY OR JUST DON'T EAT OR DRINK. I WAS DRINKING DIET DRINKS FOR A WHILE, NOT KNOWING SOME OF THE MEDS I WAS ON WERE MAKING ME KEEP MY WEIGHT ON. EVERYBODY WHO TRYS TO LOSE WEIGHT KNOWS HOW HARD IT IS TO LOSE. BUT SOMETHING THAT HELPS YOU NOT TO LOSE, ANYWAY THE POINT I WAS GETTING TO I WAS DRINKING DIET DRINKS TO HELP LOSE WEIGHT, THEN NOTICE I WAS HAVING MORE STOMACH TROUBLE, TURNS OUT IT WAS THE DRINKS, SOMETHING USED TO SWEETEN XXXXX, I COULDN'T TAKE. LOOK AT YOUR DIET DRINK FOR NAME. THEN LOOK UP THE SWEETNER, YOU WILL NOT LIKE WHEN YOU SEE THE THINGS IT DOES, OR CAN DO.

I SEEM TO BE MORE PRONE TO GETING SICK NOW, I TOLD MY DOCTOR I WAS MORE SINSITIVE TO THINGS I NEVER WAS BEFORE, WELL THIS WAS SIDE AFFECTS OF THE MEDS.

I WAS GIVEN BRAND—### ONE TIME AND IT DID HELP, BUT STARTED HAVING A SORE THROAT FROM USE, SO I HAD TO STOP TAKING. I AM JUST MORE SINSITIVE TO EVERYTHING IT SEEMS, FROM MEDS TO EVEN THINGS I WAS NEVER BOTHERED BY, ITS IN HERE A BEE STING. I KNOW PEOPLE HAVE DIED FROM A BEE STING, ONE LOCAL GUY WAS SUNG AND RUN OFF THE ROAD BUT DIED FROM THE STING. WHEN I GOT STUNG THE FIRST TIME I DIDN'T KNOW WHAT WAS GOING ON, THE

BACK OF MY THROAT FELT LIKE IT WAS SWELLING, AND WAS HARD TO SWALLOW. I WAS GIVEN SOMETHING AND WENT HOME. THEN THE DOCTOR GIVE ME A PRECRIPTION FOR THAT FAMOUS NEEDLE. I NEVER USED IT BUT IF YOU READ WHAT WILL HAPPEN IF YOU USE IT WHEN YOU DON'T NEED IT YET, WELL THAT WILL WORRY YOU. MAKE SURE YOU ARE ABOUT TO DIE, BECAUSE THIS CAN KILL YOU IF USED WRONG.

I ALSO FOUND OUT CERTAIN DRUGS, SOME I TOOK, CAN INCREASE A PERSON'S SUSCEPTIBILITY TO BACTERIAL INFECTIONS, AS YOU READ ABOVE AND HAD ON MY BACK, AND IN ONE OF MY VISITS TO THE HOSPITAL THERE WAS A MENTION OF BACTERIAL ON LUNGS OR IN LUNGS. THE DRUGS I TOOK WERE ALSO TO HELP ME WITH THE SIDE AFFECTS OF THE CHOLESTEROL MEDS. AND IF YOU HAVE TO TAKE THE CHOLESTEROL MEDS ALONG WITH CERTAIN OTHERS, WELL YOU JUST INCREASED YOUR CHANCE OF A HEART ATTACK, DEATH OR OTHER INJURIES.

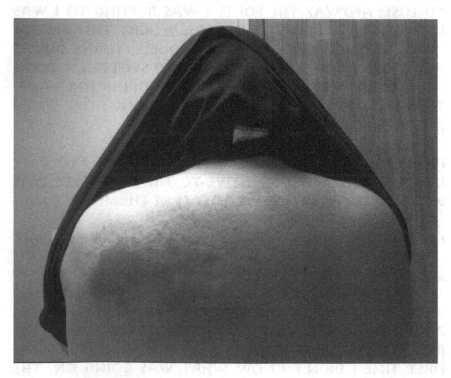

KIDNEY TROUBLES

HAD LOTS OF BLOOD IN MY URINE AND STILL HAVE TODAY. THEY SAY BECAUSE THE MEDICINE WAS IRRITATING MY KIDNEYS OR INSIDES. DON'T KNOW WHAT ESE DONE, MAYBE WORSE DON'T KNOW BUT HAVING TROUBLE NOW WAITING FOR A DOCTOR TO CHECK. HAVE HAD TROUBLE ONCE IN A WHILE NOT LIKE WHEN ON THE MEDICINE, IT WAS A WHOLE DIFFERENT THING.

HAD TO TAKE X-RAYS WITH DYE IN ME, THIS WAS ANOTHER TROUBLE? THE FIRST TIME I TOOK THE TEST WENT OK, NO TROUBLE. THE SECOND TIME I HAD A REACTION TO THE DYE USED. THEY HAD TO GIVE ME SOMETHING TO STOP THE ICHING AND SNEEZEING. ONCE AGAIN, ONLY A FEW WEEKS AFTER THE TEST WAS DONE, ON TV. HAVE YOU HAD THIS TEST DONE WITH THE DYE AND THEY GAVE A NAME. DON'T KNOW IF I TOOK THE DYE BUT IT DID CAUSE TROUBLE SOME DIDN'T SHOW UP AT THE TIME OF THE TEST FROM WHAT I UNDERSTAND. SO AGAIN I WAS EXPOSED TO TEST I HAD TO TAKE BECAUSE OF A MEDICINE THAT CAUSED MORE TROUBLE THAN THE HELP IT WAS TO DO. AND THESE ARE DANGEROUS TEST I TOOK.

I DID TRY TO GET THE NUMBER TO FIND OUT WHAT THE DYE WAS, DON'T KNOW, DIDN'T SEE ON TV ANYMORE AND DIDN'T KNOW WHAT CHANNEL WAS ON. BUT THE MAIN THING IS, THE TEST I HAD WERE CAUSED FROM SIDE AFFECTS FROM BEING ON THE CHOLESTEROL MEDICINES AND OTHERS. ANY SIDE AFFECTS ARE BECAUSE THIS MEDICINE PUT ME ON ANOTHER MEDICINE, THATS A FACT.

WOULD NOT HIRE YET!

I WAS GOING TO TRY OFFSHORE AGAIN, I WAS TOLD THE DIVE COMPANY I WENT TO WAS HIRING, I USED TO BE A ENGINER ON THE BOAT AND WANTED TO TRY AGAIN, I HAD TO DO SOMETHING I WAS USEING UP ALL MY MONEY LEFT AND RIGHT TAKING OFF FROM WORK NEEDED TO MAKE MORE PER WEEK. THE ENGINER PERSON MAINTAINS THE ENGINE AND LITE MAINTINACE ON BOAT, VERY EASY JOB UNDER NORMAL CONDITIONS. I FAILED TWO THINGS, ONE WAS BLOOD IN URINE, WHICH I WOULD HAVE TO GET A DOCTOR, TO RELEASE ME TO GO TO WORK AND FIND OUT WHY BLOOD WAS IN THERE, NEVER DID TO THIS DAY. THE OTHER WAS ONE I COULD NOT GET AWAY FROM, THE WEAKNESS IN MY HANDS I WAS TO WEAK IN MY HANDS TO HOLD ON TO A 2" ROPE FOR 30 SECONDS. THE OTHER I COULD GET BY ON BUT NOT THIS. THIS WAS INCASE I HAD TO SWING ON A ROPE FROM A RIG ON FIRE OR OTHER TO THE BOAT.

ONE MAJOR DRUG COMPANY LAWYER, DRUG 4, TOLD ME THIS DON'T CAUSE ANY TROUBLE BUT DOES CAUSE KIDNEY TROUBLE, WELL HE SAW THE MED RECORDS IF THAT DON'T TELL YOU WHAT THESE DRUGS DONE. HE DID NOT NEED ME TO TELL HIM. ALL THAT HAPPENED LED UP TO THE KIDNEY TROUBLES, AND STOMACH TROUBLES I STILL HAVE TODAY, JAN. 15,2012. THESE DRUGS ATE UP MY INSIDES, I SAW A LETTER SOMEONE HAD ON THE NET WHERE SOMEONE HAD DIED AND THE INSIDES OF THE BODY LOOKED LIKE THEY WHERE EATEN UP WITH ACID, I'AM SURE THAT'S ABOUT HOW THEY PUT IT. WHATS YOURS? IF YOU WHERE ON THESE DRUGS PLEASE DON'T GO AS LONG AS I DID. IF YOU REALIZED THAT'S WHEN YOU STARTED GETTING SICK, TELL YOUR DOCTOR, I STILL THINK I WILL END UP WITH CANCER FROM THIS, SO FAR AT LEAST 7 DRUGS I TOOK HAVE BEEN TAKEN OFF THE MARKET OR SOME KIND OF WARRING HAS BEEN PUT OUT.

SENSITIVE TO SMELLS

SMOKE FROM CIGARETTS WOULD SET ME OFF, WOULD CUT MY BREATH AWAY BAD. SOME BRANDS WOULD FEEL LIKE ITS SUCKED THE AIR OUT OF MY LUNGS AND I WOULD RUN AWAY FROM WHEN AROUND, BEFORE I WOULD PASS OUT OR DON'T KNOW WHAT WOULD HAVE HAPPENED. JUST COULD HARDLY BREATHE.

SMELLS THAT NEVER BOTHERED ME TO MUCH BEFORE SURE DID NOW!

EVEN PERFUME, COLOGNE, HOUSE CLEANERS WERE REALY BAD. GETTING GAS FOR MY TRUCK JUST FEW MONTHS AGO AND WAS HAVING TROUBLE BREATHING FOR DAYS AFTER, JUNE 2010 THIS HAPPENED. THIS WAS JUST FILLING THE GAS TANK. THAT NEVER HAPPENED BEFORE. MADE ME LIGHT HEADED & DIZZY.

THE ONLY THING HAPPENED FROM THIS THATS FUNNY, I WENT TO THE BATHROOM AND CRAPPED AND THE SMELL WAS SO BAD I THREW UP, THATS HOW SENSITIVE TO SMELLS I WAS. MY NOSE WAS NEVER LIKE THAT BEFORE. THIS NEVER HAPPENED AGAIN, WELL NOT AS OF THE TIME OF THIS WRITING. HOPE THIS NEVER HAPPENS AGAIN. I WAS LAUGHTING AND THROWING UP, FUNNY AND VOMIT DIDN'T MIX TO GOOD.

I HAD TOLD MY DOCTOR MANY TIMES THAT IT WAS LIKE EVERYTHING WAS AMPLIFIED.

SENSITIVE TO FOODS?

FOODS I ATE BEFORE THAT DID NOT BOTHER ME, DO NOW. CHINESE FOOD, TOLD THE MSG IS HIGH IN THERE FOOD AND ANY PROCESSED FOOD I NOW NOTICE I HAVE TROUBLE WITH SOME, I HAVE BREATHING TROUBLE, SOMETIMES WITHIN JUST MINUTES AFTER EATING ABOUT 15-40 MINUTES.
SOME MAJOR NAME FOOD PRODUCTS I LOVE THE TASTE, ITS VERY GOOD, BUT SOMETHING IN IT. MSG? OR MAYBE THE PRESERVATIVES, DID NOT KNOW AT THIS TIME THE MEDICINE HAD MADE ME MORE SENSITIVE TO THINGS. I DO KNOW I HAVE HAD BREATHING TROUBLE AND NOTICE SOME ANXIETY. I DO KNOW I MAKE NOTES WHEN FEELING GOOD AND WHEN I CHANGE MOODS OR THE WAY I FEEL OR BREATHE & HEART, IF RACES OR FEELS LIKE IT DOES. ONE TIME AT THE DOCTORS OFFICE MY HEART STARTED TO RACE, OR SEEMED LIKE IT DID. I TOLD THE DOCTOR BEFORE ABOUT THIS, HE RUN TEST BUT DIDN'T FIND ANYTHING. HE SAID IT SOUNDED OK AND NORMAL. BUT AT THE SAME TIME TO ME IT FELT LIKE MY HEART WAS RACING, AND AT TIMES FELT LIKE WOULD COME OUT MY CHEST. THIS MAY HAVE BEEN WHEN I GOT THE DRUG 5 TO HELP, DON'T REMEMBER, AS I SAY OVER AND OVER, TROUBLES SEEM TO OVER LAP AND GIVE ME PROBLEMS THAT I DON'T KNOW WHATS HAPPENING TO ME. MY HEART MAY RACE FROM DRINKING STRONG TEA, IS IT CAFFINE? I NOW BUY CAFFINE FREE JUST TO MAKE SURE. SOME FOODS MAKE MY CHEST FEEL LIKE THERES SOMEONE SITTING ON, SOME MAKE HEART RACE & HARD TO BREATHE. I DID REALIZE THAT FOOD SEASONINGS MESS WITH ME, I USED A LOT AT ONE TIME. DON'T USE ANY MORE, IF I GO OUT SOMEWHERE I JUST HOPE THEY DON'T USE TO MUCH SEASONS AND SPICES. THE ONLY SEASON I SEEM TO BE OK WITH IS SALT. I'LL USE BUT STILL NOT TO MUCH, JUST A PINCH. FROM THE BOTTOM

OF THE SHAKER, HA HA JUST KIDDING STILL USE LITELY. I JUST READ RECENTLY ONE OF THE MEDICINES I WAS ON SIDE AFFECTS WAS SENSATIONS OF HEART RACING.

I ATE SOME RASBERRY STUFFED DONUTS AND HAD SOME TROUBLE, THEY TASTE GREAT BUT SEEM TO HAVE HAD ANXIETY ATTACKS OR JUST NOT FEEL RIGHT.

WISH I COULD DOCTOR MY SELF FOR EACH DAY I WOULD DRAW BLOOD & AFTER EATING EACH THING THAT BOTHERED ME DRAW BLOOD AGAIN, THEN SEE WHAT SHOWS UP. NO DOCTOR WANTS TO HEAR MEDICINES MESSED YOU UP, EXSPECIALY IF THEY ARE THE ONES THAT GIVE IT TO YOU. SOME JUST SAY LETS TRY SOMETHING ESE, OR I WOULD'NT GIVE YOU ANYTHING LIKE THAT ANY MORE. THIS IS WHAT I WOULD LIKE TO HEAR, THAT YES I NOTICED SOME OF MY PEOPLE HAD THE SAME TROUBLE, I'LL MAKE A NOTE ABOUT THAT, AND SEE HOW MANY ARE HAVING THE SAME TROUBLE.

I SAID I USE SALT STILL EARLYER, DURING THE WHOLE TIME I WAS ON THE MEDS I CRAVED SALT & FELT BETTER AFTER EATING SOMETIMES. I LATER FOUND OUT I HAD SIGNS OF LOW POTASSIOM AND DIDN'T KNOW, IN MY OWN RESEARCH I FOUND MOST OF THE WEARD THINGS THAT HAPPENED TO ME WERE MEDICINE RELATED. MANY MEDICINES TAKE AWAY THINGS FROM YOUR BODY, THIS MADE ME UNDERSTAND WHY I HAD SOME OF THE TROUBLES AND WEAKNESSES.

I ALSO FOUND OUT THERE WAS A PUBLIC HEALTH ADVISORY WARNING THAT TAKING SOME OF THE DRUGS I WAS ON CAN INCREASE THE RISK OF FOOD POISONINGS. THERE WAS A COMPLANT OF THIS IN OHIO AND LAWSUIT, DID NOT SAY WHAT BRAND OF DRUG BUT WAS A STOMACH ACID REDUCER DRUG, AND ANOTHER DRUG I TOOK, WHY, BECAUSE THE CHOLESTEROL MEDS WERE MESSING WITH MY STOMACH. WHY THIS NEVER COMES TO THE PEOPLE WHO TOOK THIS STUFF AT THE TIME THEY ARE TRING TO GET HELP AND NO

ONE KNOWS WHATS WRONG WITH YOU UNTILL ITS TO LATE, THE DAMAGE IS DONE, I NOW HAVE WEAKNESS, AND OTHER HEALTH TROUBLE BECAUSE NO ONE LET ME KNOW WHAT TROUBLES TO LOOK FOR. I MEAN ALL TROUBLES. I'VE HEARD AND YOU HAVE TO, THERE MAY BE OTHER TROUBLES WITH A DRUG. WELL WHEN I ASK FOR THESE TROUBLES WAS NEVER TOLD. I HAD CALLED ONE COMPANY AND ASKED WHAT CAN I EXPECT. I WAS ONLY ASKED HAVE I EVER PASSED OUT.

OTHER PEOPLE SAME TROUBLES'

ONE OF MY AUNTS TOLD ME SHE HAD SOME OF THE SAME PROBLEMS ONE DAY, WE HADN'T TALKED IN A WHILE I HAD WHEN TO VISIT, SHE ASKED HOW I WAS DOING I TOLD HER WAS HURTING AND IT WAS BECAUSE OF THE MED I WAS ON, I TOLD HER ITS THE CHOLESTEROL MEDS AND THE OTHERS. AFTER I FINISHED TELLING HER ABOUT THE DOCTOR DIDN'T SEEM TO BELIEVE ME, SHE HAD TEARS IN HER EYES, I ASKED WHAT WAS WRONG, SHE SAID SHE HAD ALL THE WEARD ACHES AND PAINS ALSO AND IT MADE HER FEEL NOT RIGHT IN THE HEAD, WEAK, SHE WAS SO WEAK AT TIMES SHE DIDN'T KNOW WHAT TO DO. I TOLD HER MORE ABOUT OTHER TROUBLES, WE WERE HAVING ALMOST THE SAME EXTACT PROBLEMS, AFTER A WHILE I HUGED HER AND TOLD HER ONE MORE THING, I SAID I WAS TOLD THIS WEAKIN'S THE KIDNEYS AND SHES DIABETIC, AND SHE SHOULD NOT BE ON BECAUSE OF THE PROBLEMS IT CAUSES TO THE KIDNEYS, A FEW WEEKS WENT BY AND I WENT OVER AND TALKED AGAIN, SHE HAD GOT OFF OF THE CHOLESTEROL MED'S AND WASN'T AS WEAK ALL THE TIME, THAT WAS ABOUT YEAR AGO, LAST TIME WE TALKED ABOUT THIS SHE WAS DOING BETTER, STILL WEAK BUT NOT AS WEAK, SHE IS ON A BREATHING MACHINE AT NIGHT, THE SAME TYPE OF MACHINE MY DOCTOR WANT'S ME ON FOR SLEEP APNEA. THIS HELPS YOU SLEEP BETTER, WHEN YOU CAN BREATH BETTER, YOU SLEEP BETTER. I HAVE HAD BREATHING TROUBLE BECAUSE OF THE MEDICNE ALSO, ONE DOCTOR SAID I HAVE C.O.P.D. <u>THERE IS NO TURNAROUND FOR THAT</u>, AT LEAST THATS WHAT I'AM TOLD.

SO WHATS NEXT? I DON'T KNOW. FROM THE TIME I STARTED THE MEDICINES TILL I STOPPED I'VE HAD TROUBLE AND LOTS OF PERMANENT PROBLEMS, AT LEAST SOME HAVE WEAKENED,

BUT THEY ALL SEEM TO BE THERE WHEN YOU THINK ITS GONE, THERE IT IS # 2 OR # 4 ON MY LIST, IS THIS HOW I SHOULD LIST, MAYBE. I TAKE THE #2 TODAY AND CHECK BLOOD LEVELS AND PUT OFF THE #4 HARD TO BREATH FOR A WHILE.

AFTER I WROTE THE ABOVE, MY AUNT HAD TO GET ON DIALYSIS TREATMENT AND IS ON THIS AS OF THIS WRITING AUG 30, 2010. SHE ALSO HAS TO BE ON A BREATHING MACHINE TO HELP HER SLEEP APNEA. SHE TO WAS ON THE LIQUID DIET YEARS AGO AND HER SON, BOTH LIKE ME ENDED UP ON HIGH BLOOD PRESURE MEDICINE. THIS WAS BACK IN THE MID TO LATE 80S IF I REMEMBER RIGHT.

JUST RECENTLY MY AUNT TOLD ME SHE HAD ANOTHER OF THE SAME TROUBLES. I HAD DROPPED AT WORK LIKE I PASSED OUT, COULD NOT MOVE BUT WAS AWHERE OF WHAT WAS GOING ON AROUND ME, I JUST COULD NOT MOVE. SHE TOLD ME SHE WAS SITTING IN A CHAIR AND WAS WANTING TO GET UP AND JUST COULD NOT MOVE, HER BODY WOULD NOT LET HER MOVE. SHE TOLD MY UNCLE SHE COULD NOT MOVE A MUSCLE, YET WAS AWHERE OF WHAT WAS GOING ON. THIS IS A HORRIABLE FEELING, I KNOW IT HAPPEN TO ME. MAYBE YOUR READING AND SAID, YEA ME TO. THE OTHERS, WELL, YOUR LUCKY.

TODAY I WAS TOLD 3 DOCTORS HAD HER ON 3 DIFFERENT CHOLESTEROL MEDICINES, I WAS TOLD MANY TIMES THIS MEDICINE IS NOT GOOD FOR THE KIDNEY, IS THIS WHY HER KIDNEY GIVE OUT? THE TIME LINE FALLS OUT RIGHT FROM WHAT I HEARD. THE KIDNEYS SEEM TO GET WORSE OVER TIME, AND SHE WAS GIVEN THE MEDS OVER TIME. WHEN WE TALKED ABOUT THE WEAKNESS, THAT'S WHEN SHE HAD GOT OFF. SHE IS NOT AS WEAK NOW, BUT NOW HER KIDNEY GAVE OUT, SO WHOS PAYING HER FOR TAKING HER HEALTH AND KIDNEY AWAY FROM HER? <u>NO ONE</u>.

SHE GIVE HER LIFE TO TEACHING, AND RETIRES IN HER 60S. SHE WAS IN HER 20S WHEN SHE STARTED TEACHING SECOND

GRADERS. THERE A TRIP, I KNOW I'VE BEEN TO HER CLASS A FEW TIMES.

STEP MOTHER

MY STEPMOTHER HAD ALSO TAKEN CHOLESTEROL MEDS, SHE HAD MEMORY TROUBLE ALREADY FROM DEMENTIA SHE TOLD ME ONE TIME SHE HAD BEEN HAVING LOTS OF MUSCLE ACHES, STOMACH TROUBLE, AND JOINT PAINS, BUT SHE WAS ALSO FIGHTING CANCER, HER BREAST CANCER HAD COME BACK, SHE HAD A LOT ON HER PLATE BESIDES WORRING ABOUT SIDE AFFECTS OF MEDICINES, SHE DIED LAST YEAR.

GETING BACK TO MEDS, I WAS TOLD BY A FEW PEOPLE THEY HAD TROUBLE WITH RED MEAT, I DID TO I TEND TO EAT MORE CHICKEN OR PORK, DON'T KNOW WHY MAYBE THE SHOTS THEY GIVE THE ANIMALS, I DO KNOW I ALSO HAD TROUBLE WITH MILK AS I SAY HERE, AND WENT TO ORGANIC, I DID FIND SOME MEAT THAT WAS RAISED THIS WAY, DON'T REMEMBER GETING SICK. THIS DID NOT STOP ME FROM EATING, I STILL ATE MEAT JUST NOT AS OFTEN. I WAS JUST SO MESSED UP, WAS TRYING TO DETERMINE JUST WHAT WAS MESSING ME UP. I MIGHT GO FOR FEW DAYS OK, THEN BAM, SICK. I DO KNOW A LOT OF MY TROUBLES WAS MY BOWELS NOT WORKING RIGHT. WHEN YOU HEAR THE OLD SAYING, TAKE A GOOD CRAP YOU'LL FEEL BETTER, THERE RIGHT. THESE DRUGS AND PAIN PILLS MESSED THAT UP. I STILL HAVE TROUBLE TODAY WITH MY DIGESTIVE SYSTEM.

I WILL NOT SAY TO MUCH ON THIS ONE BECAUSE I CAN ALMOST TALK TO I PERSON A DAY AND FIND SOMEONE WHO IS HAVING OR HAD TROUBLE WITH CHOLESTEROL MEDICINE. ON OCT 25, 2010 SITTING DOWN EATING BREAKFAST I HAD A PERSON NEXT TO ME I SEE ALL THE TIME AT WORK, HAPPEN TO SAY HE WAS TAKING THE CHOLESTEROL MEDICINE AND THE DOCTOR GIVE HIM A HIGHER DOSE NOW HE HAS MUSCLE PAINS. I TOLD HIM TO TELL HIS DOCTOR WHAT HAPPENED, I ALSO TOLD HIM OF MINE I BELIEVE WENT ON TO LONG BECAUSE NOW I HAVE PERMANENT MUSCLE TROUBLE, EVERY

SINCE I PASSED OUT OR LOST MOTOR CONTROL I NEVER GOT MY STRENGH BACK.

HE TOLD ME HIS DAD WAS ABOUT 89 OR 90 AND TOOK NO MEDICINES.

OCT 25, 2010 NEXT DAY WENT TO LOCAL AUTO STORE TO PICK UP POINTS FOR MY BOAT AND PAY FOR MY UNCLES' BATTERY, HIS WIFE MY AUNT TALKED ABOUT IN THIS BOOK WAS PUT IN THE HOSPITAL AND JUST GIVEN MORE MEDICINES, BLOOD THINNERS.

I TOLD HIM TO MAKE SURE SHE TELLS THE DOCTOR IF SHE HAS ANY STOMACH TROUBLE. THIS WAS THE SAME MEDICINE MY DAD WAS ON, MY STEP DAD, AND MY MOTHER AND AT ONE POINT ALL HAD SOME KIND OF STOMACH TROUBLE. GOT AWAY THERE BUT AGAIN EVERYDAY SEEMS TO BE TROUBLE WITH ME OR SOMEONE I KNOW ON MEDS THAT MAY BE TO STRONG OR TAKEN TO LONG GIVE SOME KIND OF TROUBLE. GETING BACK TO WHILE IN THE STORE, THE OWNER WAS TALKING TO SOMEONE AND MYSELF, HE STARTED TALKING ABOUT HIS MEDS AND BEING WEAK A LOT BUT MOSTLY WEAKNESS. WHEN IT WAS ALL OVER HE TOLD US OF HIS MEDS AND HAVING TROUBLES, BUT HE SEEM TO NOTE THAT MOST THINGS HAPPENED AFTER THE LAST MEDICINE HE WAS ON. YOU GUESSED IT, CHOLESTEROL MEDICINE. I'AM NOT A DOCTOR BUT I CAN SEE THE COMMON THING HERE FOR TROUBLE. HE ALSO NOTED HE WAS CONSTIPATED A LOT, AND SOMETHING I SAID LONG TIME AGO, HE NOTED HE AND HIS NURSE SAID IT WAS GETTING HARDER TO FIND HIS VIENS. WONDER WHY!!!

IS THIS STUFF MAKING IT HARDER TO FIND. OR STRINKING THE VIENS LIKE I SAY, IF YOU LOOK IN THE BOOK LATER YOU WILL SEE WHERE ONE DOCTOR NOTED A THICKING OF MY BLADDER WALL, (THIS IS DATED 4/11/2005 IN NOTES FROM MY DOCTOR) WHY NOT OTHER THINGS IN MY BODY ITS THE ONLY THING THAT MAKES ANY SENCE FOR WHAT HAPPENED

TO ME AND OTHERS THAT I KNOW ABOUT, AND THIS IS THE 3RD PERSON THAT NOTICED THE SAME THING.

THERE WAS ALSO ONE OF MY X-RAYS I REMEMBER SOMEONE SAYING IT LOOKED LIKE I HAD ENLARGED ORGANS OR LARGER THAN NORMAL AT THAT TIME.

THEN THERES THE SIDE AFFECT THING. ONE OF THE MEDICNES CAN ENLARGE BODY ORGANS.

TODAY NOVEMBER 13, 2010, WENT TO THE FLYING FIELD, WHERE REMOTE CONTROL PLANES ARE FLOWN, JUST AS I KEEP SAYING I CAN FIND ONE PERSON A DAY WITHOUT EVEN TRYING THAT IS HAVING SOME KIND OF CHOLESTEROL MEDICINE TROUBLE. THEY TOLD ME OF WEAKNESS AND JUST STARTING OF JOINT PAIN. HE WAS ON FOR ABOUT ONE YEAR. MAYBE IN THE NEXT BOOK OR A UPDATED VERSION OF THIS ONE IN ABOUT 2-5 YEARS IF I'AM STILL AROUND, I WILL GET A NOTEBOOK AND LET EACH PERSON SIGN AND GIVE A LITTLE OF THERE TROUBLES. I THINK I WOULD HAVE THE NOTEBOOK FULL IN NO TIME FLAT.

THE PERSON I TALKED TO ABOUT THIS DID SAY HE'D TRYED TO KEEP TAKING BECAUSE HE DIDN'T KNOW WHAT TO DO. I TOLD HIM CHANGE HIS DIET, IF HE DON'T WANT TO SUFFER WITH MEDICINES. I ALSO TOLD HIM WHAT I WAS TOLD, IF YOUR MUSCLES ARE HURTING, GET OFF OF THIS STUFF!! YOU MAY BE LUCKLY AND HAVE NO MUSCLE OR JOINT DAMAGE LIKE I HAVE. YOU READ OR WILL READ THAT ONE COMPANYS LAWYER TOLD ME THIS. WHY DO DOCTORS STILL GIVE OUT? WHY IS THIS A MAKE YOU SUFFER WORLD. LAWS FOR THINGS TO TAKE YOUR RIGHTS AWAY, SOME BECAUSE ONLY A FEW PEOPLE MAY HAVE GOT HURT ON SOMETHING SO LETS MAKE EVERYBODY NOT HAVE FUN, I TELL THEM NOT EVERYBODYS DRUNK OR NOT SAFE. HERE'S A GOOD ONE MY NEPHEW POPED SOME FIRE CRACKERS ONE NIGHT AND GOT ARESTED FOR DOING THIS. THE FOURTH OF JULY IS INDEPENDENCE DAY FOR FREEDOM. A YOUNG KID GOT HURT SO THE TOWN

BANNED. I'AM SORRY FOR THE YOUNG KID, BUT BE REAL, HE SHOULD NOT HAVE HAD THE FIRE CRACKER, A GROWN ADULT NOT DRUNK AND USES SAFE ACTIONS, SHOULD BE ABLE TO POP AT LEAST SOME OF THE SMALLER STUFF.

HERES ANOTHER ONE EVERY ONE WANTS TO MAKE SURE THERE KIDS DON'T DO ANYTHING BAD. BUT LAWMAKERS IN SOME AREAS FINE THE KID HIGH FINES FOR SMOKING. BELIEVE ME I DON'T WANT ANY KID TO SMOKE OR START. BUT THE PARENTS ARE THE ONES WHO WILL PAY THESE FINES AND SUFFER AND SOME I KNOW CAN'T AFFORD, I KNOW FIRST HAND THIS HAPPENED IN MY FAMILY. ITS NOT LIKE THEY DONE SOMETHING REALY BAD FOR A FINE SO HIGH. WHY WE CAN'T FINE THE PEOPLE IN OFFICE, WHEN THEY SPEND OUR TAX DOLLARS LIKE THERE'S NO END AND WANT MORE. THERES ALWAYS SEEM TO BE MONEY FOR RAISES BUT NOT 300.00 POT HOLE. THATS WHATS GOING ON NOW, JUST TAX US WITHOUT MY CONSENT. WE HAVE TO PAY BECAUSE ITS THE LAW NOW, I HEAR PEOPLE IN THE GOVERMENT SAY THIS A LOT, THE WASTE NEEDS TO STOP. THERE NEEDS TO BE A SET SALARY, YOU DON'T LIKE, DON'T RUN. IF THERE ARE ANY RAISES, ITS BASED ON THAT PART OF THE GOVERMENT DOING THERE JOB NOT WASTING MONEY, THEN MAYBE A BONUS. YOU KNOW LIKE IN THE REAL WORLD. IN THE REAL WORLD YOU SHOW YOU CAN SAVE MONEY IN A BUSSINESS, YOU GET A SMALL BONUS OR A—DA—BOY, YOUR DOING GOOD. REPUBLICANS AND DEMOCRATS. THIS IS THE REAL WORLD, DON'T EVEN SAY WE SHOULD DO THIS OR THAT, BUT CAN'T BECAUSE WHERE NOT IN POWER NOW, THE BLAME GAME, BUT WHEN YOU WHERE IN POWER YOU DID NOT DO ANYWAY. THE PEOPLE ARE TIRED OF THIS. ONE REPUBLICAN WAS ON TV FEW DAYS AGO DOING JUST THIS, I DON'T KNOW ABOUT YOU, BUT I HAVE SEEN THIS ON BOTH SIDES OF THE POLITICAL ARENA. PLEASE WORK TOGETHER, THIS IS NOT FOR YOU, BUT THE PEOPLE WHO PUT YOU IN THAT OFFICE AND DON'T EVER FORGET THAT.

HOW DOES THIS FIT IN WITH ALL MY TROUBLE. THEY WANT TO CUT MONEY TO HOSPITALS THAT ARE OVER TAKEN BY SICK PEOPLE, SOME LIKE ME THAT WHERE PUT THERE BECAUSE OF MEDICINES, AND SHOULD HAVE NOT BEEN USED UNTILL FURTHER TESTING. <u>FDA NEEDS TO BE MORE ACCOUNTABLE AND JOBS LOST</u>. IF THEY DON'T READ ALL THE DATA AT LEAST I SAY TALK TO THE TESTED PEOPLE DIRECTLY I DON'T CARE IF ITS 2000 PEOPLE, IF NOT A LONG TERM USE MED IS ONE THING, BUT ALL MEDICINES USED LONG TERM THE TAKERS SHOULD BE FOLLOWED LONG TERM. AND LONG TERM DATA, AND NOT YEARS LATER, WELL WE CHANGED OUR MINDS, WE THINK THIS IS TO BAD. LETS PULL OFF THE MARKET THIS OR THAT DRUG AFTER ITS DONE TO MUCH DAMAGE, WHEN THIS HAPPENS TO YOU, YOU'LL KNOW HOW I FELT AND OTHERS, AND FEEL SORRY FOR THE ONES WHO DIDN'T MAKE IT. LIKE ONE DRUG I WAS ON, KNOWN FOR HEART ATTACKS, I TOLD MY DOCTOR I JUST NEW I WAS HAVING A HEART ATTACK I COULD FEEL MY BLOOD PULSEING IN MY NECK, SKIN PULLED DOWN OVER MY HEAD, HEART NOT FEELING RIGHT, AFTER I TOOK MY SELF OFF DRUG1 AND 1B THEY WHERE ON TV FOR HEART ATACKS AND MEDICAL TROUBLES. DOCTORS WAKE UP, TAKE THE TIME TO MAKE A NOTE AND CALL THE DRUG COMPANYS OR AT LEAST WRITE TO THEM, AGAIN I WROTE AND CALLED THE FDA, NO CALL BACKS. THESE WERE INFLAMITORY DRUGS

TODAY DEC. 23, 2011, ONE OF MY MOTHERS FRIENDS TOLD US TWO OF HER RELITIVES HAD TO GET OFF THESE DRUGS, AGAIN, I CAN ALMOST FIND SOMEONE EVERYDAY WITH CHOLESTEROL MED HORRORS.

AS I SAID, EVERY TIME I HAD TO EDIT THE BOOK I PUT IN A NEW PERSON THAT IS HAVING TROUBLE, TODAY IS DEC. 25, 2011 AND A CHRISTMAS HOLIDAY, I'AM WANTING TO GO TO DOCTOR WOKE UP WITH KIDNEY PAINS ON MY LEFT SIDE, I STILL BURN IN SIDE THE DOCTOR SAID I HAD A BAD ULCER THAT WAS REACURING, AND YOU KNOW WHAT HAPPENS WHEN SOMETHING STAYS RAW

TO LONG, I STILL HAVE TROUBLE WITH MSGS, PRESERVATIVES, AND NOT BEING ABLE TO KNOW WHATS GOING TO HAPPEN IS A HORROR, WILL IT GET BETTER, SO FAR DON'T LOOK LIKE IT. EACH TIME EAT MEAT, MY JOINTS HURT, I TRY TO STAY AWAY FROM MEAT BUT ONCE IN A WHILE I'AM ON THE ROAD AND GET HUNGERY BURGER OR CHICKEN? CHICKEN AROUND THIS AREA IS FULL OF PEPPER, BURGER OR SANDWICH IS BETTER, EVEN THE TOPINGS BOTHER ME SOMETIMES, PERSERVATIVES IN THEM IS ALL I CAN GUESS.

PASSED OUT AT WORK

THIS HAPPENED ONE WEEKEND, RIGHT AFTER I HAD CALLED THE DRUG COMPANY DRUG 1 OF THE STATIN DRUG LINE. I HAD TOLD THEM OF MY TROUBLES AND AFTER A WHILE ON THE PHONE HE NEW MY TROUBLES WERE FROM THE MEDICINE. ONE OF THE FIRST THINGS HE ASKED ME, WAS DID YOU EVER PASS OUT? AT THAT TIME I TOLD HIM NO. BUT I DID ABOUT 1 WEEK LATER, I HAD STOPPED TAKING THE MEDICINE AND WAS STILL HAVING TROUBLE BUT WAS STARTING TO WEAKEN.

I NEVER GOT MY STRENGH BACK. ABOUT ONE MAYBE TWO WEEKS LATER, I WAS LAYING ON THE FLOOR. IT WAS LIKE I HAD MELTED ON TO THE FLOOR JUST STARTED GETTING WEAK FAST, I REMEMBER REACHING OUT TO GRAB SOMETHING TO KEEP ME FROM DROPPING TO THE FLOOR BUT KEPT GOING DOWN, ONCE ON THE FLOOR I ONLY REMEMBER LAYING ON MY SIDE, NOT BEING ABLE TO MOVE AT ALL!!, JUST MY EYES, I COULD SEE THE PROJECTOR, I COULD HEAR, COULD NOT EVEN TALK OR YELL, I JUST KNEW I WAS DIEING OR WORSE, BUT DIDN'T EVEN KNOW WHAT. WHAT SEEMS LIKE FOR EVER, I KEPT TRYING TO MOVE, MY MIND SAID MOVE, BUT I COULD NOT MOVE. I LAID STILL FOR A WHILE. I WAS THINKING OF MY DAD AND UNCLE THEY HAD PASSED AWAY AND NEW I WOULD BE WITH THEM AND OTHER FAMILY MEMBERS, THEN THERE WAS LIKE A SHOCK IN MY CHEST AREA, AND I MOVED MY LEG A LITTLE. THEN I SLOWLY STARTED TO BE ABLE TO MOVE. I GOT UP WENT TO SIT DOWN. AFTER ABOUT 5 MINUTES IT WAS LIKE NOTHING EVER HAPPENED. (I WANT TO NOTE THIS IS NOT THE FIRST TIME I HAD SOME KIND OF SHOCK, ITS LIKE MY HEART WOULD JUMP WHEN I WOULD GET THESE SHOCKS) I SHOULD HAVE WENT TO THE HOSPITAL, BUT ALL THE TEST THEY HAD BEEN RUNNING THEY SAY NOTHINGS

WRONG. DID TELL MY DOCTOR, DON'T REMEMBER WHAT HE SAID. DON'T KNOW IF YOU WOULD CALL THIS PASSING OUT OR JUST WHAT, I DID REMEMBER GOING DOWN, DON'T REMEMBER HOW LONG DOWN, BUT WAS A WHILE, IT WAS LIKE SOME ONE TURNED OFF A SWITCH AND I LOST ALL ABILITY TO STAND AND MOVE, ITS NOT THE FIRST TIME. ONE TIME WAS WALKING AND LEFT LEG GIVE OUT, LIKE TURNING A SWITCH OFF AND ON, I STARTED TO GO DOWN AND THEN COME BACK UP. THIS MESSED WITH MY LIFE ALL THE TIME. IT IS SO HARD TO SAY IN WORDS BUT HOPE NO ONE HAS TO GO THROUGH THIS, WELL MAYBE THE PEOPLE WHO WANT TO MAKE THESE DRUGS TAKEN BY EVERY ONE EVEN IF YOU DON'T NEED. I SAW THIS ON TV, THE GOVERMENT AND DRUG COMPANYS MESSING UP YOUR LIFES AND WHEN YOU CAN'T WORK AND THEY WANT TO TAKE YOUR HOUSE OR CAR AWAY, WELL SO, ITS YOUR TROUBLE NOW. THIS IS HOW I SEE IT, WHEN I STARTED HAVING TROUBLE, THIS IS HOW I WAS TREATED. I DID TRY TO DRAW DISABILITY, I COULD NOT BECAUSE I HAD LAND FROM MY DADS DEATH, AND A LITTLE MONEY BUT USED THIS TO LIVE ON WHEN I COULD NOT WORK, I USED MOST OF THAT TO LIVE ON AND BOUGHT SOME LAND FROM MY STEP MOTHER, BUT NOW I HAVE LESS MONEY ALMOST DOWN TO 3,000.00 AND THEY WANT THAT. YOU HAVE TO BE BROKE BEFORE THEY HELP. YOU CAN'T HAVE A LITTLE BACK UP MONEY. I LOST A LOT OF MONEY FROM THIS WHOLE MESS, DOCTORS, TIME LOST AT WORK, AND MORE MY HEALTH. YOU'LL READ ABOUT I TRYED TO PUT AS MUCH AS I CAN IN THIS BOOK.

AGAIN, I'AM I DIEING? I JUST KNOW AS TIME WENT ON, I HAD LESS INTENCE TROUBLE. BUT NEVER GOT OVER THE WEAKNESS, I STILL HAVE TROUBLE TODAY, BUT LEARNED TO LIVE WITH, BUT THE MENTAL AFFECTS ARE SOMETHING BEYOND WHAT I CAN ONLY TRY TO DISCRIBE, WHEN I TRY TO TALK ABOUT THIS I SOMETIMES CRY, THIS BRINGS BACK ALL THE HORROR I HAD. I'VE BEEN CRING FOR HELP AND THE DOCTOR THAT RUNS TEST DON'T KNOW WHAT ESE TO RUN. THE DRUG COMPANY I CALLED WANTED TO GIVE ME A

COMPINSATION CHECK FOR WHAT I WAS GOING THROUGH, BUT NEVER CALLED BACK AND I LOST THE INFORMATION THEY GAVE ME. BUT WHAT HE TOLD ME WOULD SHOCK YOU.

NO ONE OVER 50 SHOULD BE ON THIS MEDICINE, THE FIRST SIGN OF MUSCLES ACHING, THE DOCTOR SHOULD HAVE STOPPED. I HAD TOLD HIM MY DOCTOR HAD LOOKED UP ON THE NET IN FRONT OF ME AND HE TOLD ME THE MEDICINE SHOULD NOT BE DOING THIS, THATS WHY I KEPT TAKING, MY BODY SAID NO, I WAS THINKING NO, BUT LISTENED TO MY DOCTOR AND NOT MY BODY!

THIS IS WHY I WROTE THIS BOOK. YOU KNOW YOUR OWN BODY, LISTEN TO WHAT IT TELLS YOU ANYTHING OUT OF NORMAL MAKE NOTE'S, THIS DOES HELP. AT ONE POINT WHEN I WAS ON MANY OF THESE DRUGS I DIDN'T KNOW WHICH WAS GIVING ME WHAT TROUBLE. AS I SLOWLY GOT OFF EACH DRUG, I DID NOTICE CHANGES. MOST TO THE BETTER. I EVEN STOPPED TAKING MY BLOOD PRESSURE MEDICINE FOR A MONTH. I DID KEEP CHECKING MY BLOOD PRESSURE EVERY DAY AND DID OK FOR JUST AT A MONTH, BUT HAD TO GET BACK ON, AND STILL ON TODAY BUT ONLY SMALL AMOUNT 5-10 MG. I ALSO STILL STAY WEAK, I HAVE WEAK SPELLS OF MORE WEAKNESS, BUT THERES A LEVEL OF WEAKNESS THAT NEVER CHANGES.

I HAVE BEEN LOOKING UP EACH MEDICINE ON THE NET AND THEY ALL HAVE ALMOST THE SAME THING, MUSCLES SEEM TO BE THE FIRST TO GO, JOINTS, AND THEN OTHER ACHES, SOMEWHERE IN THE MID PART OF THIS MY STOMACH WAS GIVING ME TROUBLE. IF I COULD FEEL GOOD FOR JUST ONE MONTH I WOULD FEEL LIKE SOMETHING GOOD IS HAPPENING, BUT JUST WHEN YOU THINK ITS OK, BAM, SOMETHING DON'T FEEL RIGHT OR HURTING IN THE SAME SPOTS, MUSCLES AND JOINTS, AND DON'T FORGET THE DEPENDABLE STOMACH TROUBLE.

CANCER SPOTS

I HAVE HAD SPOTS LIKE A BLACK WART POPING UP ALL OVER MY ARMS. I CAN PEAL THEM OFF WITH MY FINGER NAIL SOMETIMES. I WAS TOLD THIS IS SOME TYPE OF CANCER, THEY BLEED SOMETIMES. I DON'T REMEMBER WHAT TYPE OF CANCER THEY WERE BUT THE DOCTOR DIDN'T SEEM TO THINK AT THIS TIME THEY WERE A BAD TYPE, BUT HE HASN'T CHECKED THEM OUT YET AT THE TIME OF THIS WRITING. ALSO NOTE THE PICTURE OF CANCER ON MY FOOT, WORRY ABOUT THAT LEFTED WHEN GOT OFF THE MEDICINES, BUT WILL IT COME BACK?

HAD A RASH ON MY BACK THAT FLARED UP FROM A BATH, WORRYED ABOUT THAT, SEEMS TO POP UP AT ODD TIMES, AND MY MOLD ON BACK WAS RUBBED OFF BY ME. WORRYED ABOUT THAT, BUT DOCTORS DIDN'T THINK IT WAS ANY THING TO WORRY ABOUT, MY WORRY WILL THIS LEAD TO OTHER CANCERS? OR TRAVEL TO OTHER ORGANS IN THE BODY, THE MOLD WAS NEAR MY LUNGS. I WAS TOLD A FRIEND OF MINE HAD DIED BECAUSE A MOLD TURNED CANCER AND HE DIED ABOUT YEAR LATER EVEN WITH TREATMENT.

I ALSO HAD PAINS IN SAME AREA OFF AND ON FROM LEFT TO RIGHT ON REAR SHOULDER LOWER PART. CAN ALMOST DRAW A LINE OF THE AREA'S IN A CIRCLE FROM THE FRONT ALL THE WAY AROUND TO REAR, WHEN I HURT SEEMS TO BE IN A GENERAL AREA. CENTER FRONT JUST AT THE RIB CAGE NEAR THE HEART AND MAKE A BIG CIRCLE AND YOU HAVE THE AREA.

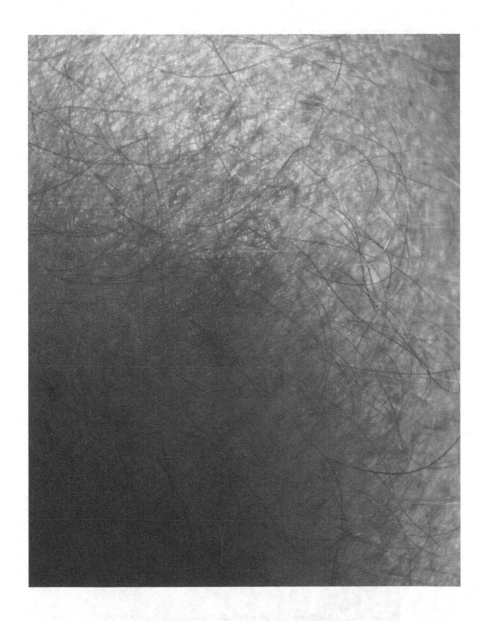

THE RASH IS GONE NOW, BUT WAS TOLD SOME KIND OF FUNGLE RASH, AGAIN THIS WAS NOTED AS SOME KIND OF SIDE AFFECT ON ONE OF THE DRUGS I TOOK. SEE THE PICTURES, I AM GLAD I TOOK SOME PICTURES OF SOME OF THE THINGS THAT HAPPENED.

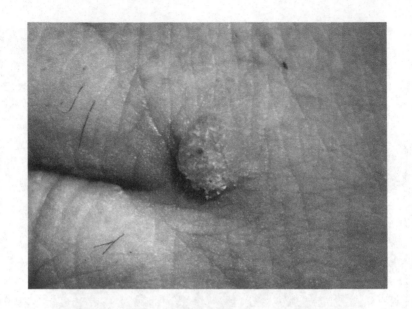

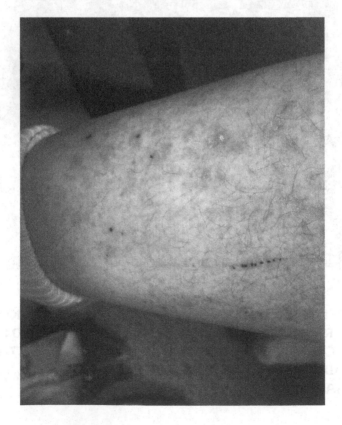

THE POINT IS I HAD A BETTER CHANCE TO HAVE A HEART ATTACK WHILE ON THESE DRUGS THAN JUST NOT TAKING. MY HEALTH RECORDS PROVE. ABOUT 2 DOCTOR VISITS A YEAR BEFORE DRUGS. AFTER TAKING DRUGS, HOSPITAL, PAIN, LOST WORK, MORE DOCTOR VISITS, MORE MEDS, MORE TEST, MORE PAIN, ABOUT 5+ YEARS OF MY LIFE GONE. OFF DRUGS, WELL DOCTOR VISITS ABOUT 2-4 TIMES A YEAR, DOWN TO ABOUT 2 PILLS ON AVERAGE, LITE PAIN EVERY DAY, WEAK EVERY DAY, BUT STILL BETTER THAN WHEN I WAS ON ALL THESE DRUGS. ALSO I HAVEN'T HAD THE HEAVYNESS IN THE LEGS HARDLY AT ALL. THATS A FACT . . . MY HEALTH HAS LEVELED OUT PERTY MUCH. NO WAY BACK TO NORMAL, BUT ABOUT AS CLOSE AS I CAN GET, SO FOR. WHEN ALL MY MUSCLE STRENGTH COMES BACK, ALL MY HEALTH PROBLEMS GO AWAY, AND I FEEL LIKE I'AM 33-44 JUST BEFORE I TOOK ALL THESE MEDS, WELL I THINK I'LL BE BACK TO NORMAL, OH YEA AND HAVE A GOOD PAYING JOB 150.00-600.00 A DAY. AS LONG AS I HAVE BEEN OFF THE MEDICINES NOW I SHOULD HAVE GOT MY STRENGH BACK, BUT SO FAR, NO.

AND THE CHOLESTEROL MEDICINE COMPANYS PAY ME WHAT THEY OWE ME. MY LIFE BACK!!!

CANCER? CHOLESTEROL MED? RELATED?

I AM NO DOCTOR BUT, I THINK SO, IN STUDYING THE CAUSE OF SOME CANCERS EVERYBODY KNOWS WHEN A SORE OR RAW SPOT ON OR IN THE BODY STAYS IRRITATED TO LONG IT CAN TURN TO CANCER. THIS IS SAID MANY TIMES, AND TOLD TO ME BY SOME OF THE DOCTORS I SAW, IN MY SEARCHS ON THE NET I FOUND THAT PANCRATIC CANCER CAN COME FROM A ULCER IN THE STOMACH, CHOLESTEROL MEDS CAUSE MANY PEOPLE TO HAVE STOMACH TROUBLES AND MAKE THEM TAKE A DRUG FOR ACID REDUCTION. I'VE TAKEN BRANS NX AND RG FOR STOMACH TROUBLES ALONG WITH OVER THE COUNTER DRUGS WHICH WORK VERY WELL, THIS IS TO HELP CUT OR SLOW DOWN ACID PRODUCTION IN THE STOMACH AND IF YOU HAVE OR HAD AN ULCER TO HELP HEAL. BUT IF YOU HAVE CONTINUOUS SORES THAT DON'T HEAL THE SEARCHS I DONE SAY THIS CAN LEAD TO CANCER OR PANCREATIC CANCER WHICH IS WHAT MY STEPDAD AND UNCLE DIED FROM. MY UNCLES DOCTOR TOLD MY AUNT IT WAS THE CHOLESTEROL MED THAT KILLED HIM BECAUSE OF WHAT IT CAUSED. I YEAR BEFORE MY STEPDAD DIED, HE HAD A BAD ULCER ATTACK. HE WAS ALSO TAKEN OFF BRAND W WHICH CAN CAUSE STOMACH TROUBLES OR ULCERS, I SEE WHY HIS STOMACH WAS SO MESSED UP HE WAS TAKEN OFF OTHERS DON'T REMEMBER WHICH ONES BUT WERE ALSO BAD ON THE STOMACH. BACK TO THE ULCER, THE DR SAID IT WAS THE SIZE OF A SAUCER, WE WERE ALSO TOLD HIS BODY WAS INFLAMED, NO ONE SAID CANCER, IT WASN'T LONG AFTER HE STARTED LOSING WEIGHT, I AM NO DOCTOR, BUT I KNEW SOMETHING WAS WRONG. NO DR NOTICED ANY THING. NOT EVEN HIS WEIGHT LOST. BUT HE HAD SAID HE DIDN'T

FEEL RIGHT AT TIMES, HE WAS ALSO TAKEN OFF OF BRAND W WHICH CAN CAUSE STOMACH TROUBLE BY ITS SELF, BUT HE DIDN'T KNOW WHAT WAS GOING ON, IN DEC. OF 2009 HE FOUND OUT HE HAD A TUMER. HE HAD TURNED YELLOW, JAUNDICE, IT WAS TO LATE, IT BLOCKED THE BILE DUCK, AND WAS CANCER AND SPREAD TO THE PANCREAS. THEY COULD MAYBE REMOVE, BUT HE WAS OLD AND WOULDN'T SURVIVE THE CHEMOTHERAPY

I MET MANY PEOPLE IN THE HOSPITAL, AND THEY TALK, THEY SAY THEY WHERE A PERFECTLY HEALTHY PERSON, AND TOOK THE SAME MEDS I TOOK. AND WHERE HAVING THE SAME . . . PROBLEMS, A FEW I TALKED TO HAD TOLD ME THEY HAD CANCER, SOME NEW WHAT TYPE PANCREATIC!!! THE COMMON MEDS WE ALL TOOK, WAS CHOLESTEROL MEDICINE AND EVEN SOME OF THE SAME OTHER MEDICINES TO COUNTER REACT THE AFFECTS. SOME LIKE ME HAD TAKEN NO OTHERS, I TAKE BLOOD PRESURE MEDICINE, BUT HAD NEVER HAD ANY TROUBLE, WHICH BY THE WAY, DRUG1. WAS NOT TO BE TAKEN WITH THE FIRST BLOOD PRESSURE MEDICINE I WAS ON, BLOOD PRESSURE MED AT 240MG, AND I WAS ON 40MG OF THE CHOLESTEROL MEDICINE, THIS WAS THE FIRST ONE I TOOK, LATER WAS PUT ON ANOTHER, AND ANOTHER UNTIL I SAID, NO MORE MEDS.

REMEMBER I AM NO DOCTOR, BUT I SAW THIS LATER. I TOLD MY DOCTOR OF THE TROUBLES OF MEDICINE, IN SOME CASES THEY WHERE ON TV ONLY 2 WEEKS AFTER I GOT OFF, FOR BAD SIDE AFFECTS SOME I WARNED MY DOCTOR MONTHS BEFORE, I THINK THERE WERE 6 OF THE MEDICINES I WAS ON WERE ON TV, FOR THE PROBLEMS I HAD.—HAVE YOU TAKEN THIS DRUG. ITS CAUSED THIS, AND WOULD HAVE A LISTOF TROUBLES, JUST LIKE WHAT I TOLD MY DOCTOR. MY TROUBLES I HAD WERE MOST ALL ON THAT LIST. SOMETIMES I WOULD NOT SEE ALL THE SAME SIDE AFFECTS ON THE LIST, BUT LATER THEY MUST HAVE REDONE, THEN YES! HEY I HAD THAT.

THESE ARE SOME MEDS I TOOK THAT WHERE ON TVS' LAWYERS LIST

BRAND—

BRAND—

BRAND—

BRAND—MANY MAJOR MAKERS OVER 7 I TOOK AND SEEMS TO BE MORE AND MORE PUT ON TV, SORRY CANT PUT NAME BUT YOU MAY HAVE SEEN ON TV.

THERES MORE THAT POP UP EVERY NOW AND THEN LIKE THE FIRST ONE I TOOK, DRUG 1 WAS A STATIN WELL KNOWN DRUG

HAD TAKEN THE DRUG3 BEFORE THE DRUG 5 BUT WAS HAVING LOTS OF MUSCLE ACHES FROM THAT AND GOT OFF. HAD TO WEED MYSELF OFF THIS. IT ALSO SEEMS, ALMOST EVERY ONE OF THE MEDS CAUSED A MUSCLE ACHE OR SOME KIND OF A PAIN, OR DAMAGE TO MY BODY SOMEWHERE. I HAVE BEEN OFF THE MEDS FOR OVER 2 YEARS, I STILL HAVE WEAKNESS!! AND PAIN!!

TREMORS & MORE

I BELIEVE THAT IT WAS YEAR 2 OF THE TROUBLE ON MEDICINE, I WAS AT MY MOTHERS HOUSE WE WERE TALKING AND JUST RELAXING, I JUST STARTED SHAKING, LEFT TO RIGHT FOR A FEW SECONDS I NEW I WAS SHAKING AND COULD NOT STOP, I DIDN'T PASS OUT, I WAS SHOCKED, I LOOKED AT MY MOTHER AND STEPDAD AND SAID MAMA, I THINK I'AM GETTING OR HAVE PARKINSONS, THIS IS WHAT THEY SAID MAMA HAD. THIS WAS THE FIRST TIME THIS HAD HAPPENED TO ME, THERE WERE A FEW OTHERS LATER BUT NOT AS BAD AS THIS ONE. JUST ABOUT 2 DAYS LATER I SAW A GIRL I WORKED WITH AND WE STARTED TALKING, SHE TOLD ME SHE WAS ON THE SAME MEDICINE I WAS ON AND SHE HAD TO GET OFF, SHE WAS HAVING TREMORS, I LOOKED AT HER AND SAID I DID TO. I HAD STOPPED TAKING ALL MY MEDS BUT THE BLOOD PRESSURE AFTER THAT. BY THIS TIME I WAS ON THE 3RD TYPE OF CHOLESTEROL MEDICINE. I'AM NOT SURE OF THE ORDER OF THINGS BUT I TRY TO PUT IN THE ORDER THAT EVERY THING HAPPENED.

MY MOTHER WAS ALSO ON THE CHOLESTEROL MEDS. DON'T REMEMBER WHICH ONE AT THAT TIME, BUT I DO REMEMBER THERE WAS A TIME WHEN WE SAW MORE SHAKING THAN NORMAL FROM HER, WHICH MAKES ME THINK, WAS THIS MAKING HER SHAKE WORSE. I THINK SO. THERES MANY TIMES SHE GOT NEW MEDS TO TRY, AND I NOTICED NEW TROUBLES, HER DOCTOR RE-AJUSTED HER MEDS, AND SHE HAD GOT OFF OF THE CHOLESTEROL MEDS ALSO, I HAD GOT OFF FIRST WHEN I STARTED FEELING A LITTLE BETTER AND NOT GOING TO DOCTOR AS MUCH, MY STEPDAD HAD STOPPED TAKING HIS CHOLESTEROL MEDICINE, WHEN HE SAW I WAS FEELING BETTER, THEN MAMA STOP TAKING HERS' LATER. IT WAS A

FEW MONTHS LATER I TOLD MY STEPDAD, DO YOU NOTICE ANY THING? HE SAID WHAT DO YOU MEAN. I SAID NONE OF US HAD TO GO TO THE DOCTOR OR HOSPITAL SINCE WE ALL GOT OFF OF THE CHOLESTEROL MEDICINE. HE SMILED AND SAY YES. BUT WE WERE ALL STILL WEAK, BETTER BUT NOT THE SAME IS ABOUT THE BEST WAY TO SAY HOW WE FELT. OVER TIME NONE OF US EVER GOT ALL OF OUR STRENGTH BACK, BUT WENT ALMOST A YEAR WITH OUT GOING TO HOSPITAL, AND EVEN DOCTOR VISITS WHERE NOT AS MUCH.

WHEN HE DID GO TO THE HOSPITAL HE HAD THAT BAD ULCER, THE SIZE OF A SAUCER AND NOT LONG AFTER HE HAD STARTED LOSING WEIGHT. A SIGN OF CANCER BUT NOBODY SAW, IT WAS IN DECEMBER OF 2009, I WENT TO THERE HOUSE, I CHECKED ON THEM ALMOST EVERY DAY. I WALKED IN SAT DOWN, I LOOKED AT HIM TO SAY SOMETHING AND STOPPED. I LOOKED AT MAMA AND LOOKED AT MY STEPDAD, AND SAID EDGAR, YOU'RE YELLOW, HE PUT HIS HEAD DOWN AND DIDN'T SAY ANYTHING, AS IF HE DIDN'T THINK ANY ONE WOULD NOTICE.

MAMA SAID SHE WASN'T SURE IF IT WAS HER EYES OR WHAT. BUT DIDN'T SAY ANY THING THAT MORNING, AFTER FEW DAYS HE FINDLY WENT BACK TO DOCTOR AND THEY SAID HE HAD A TUMOR BLOCKING THE BILE DUCK, AND IT WAS CANCER!

I 'AM NO DOCTOR, BUT YOU KNOW WHEN SOMETHING IS SORE OR RAW TO LONG, IT CAN OR WILL TURN TO CANCER. IT WAS ONLY ABOUT 1 YEAR BEFORE HE HAD THE ULCER, AND NOT LONG AFTER HE STARTED LOSING WEIGHT. HE TO HAD STOMACH TROUBLE WHEN ON THE MEDS. HE ALSO TOOK MORE THAN I DID. AND SOME OF THE ONES HE WAS ON CAUSE'S STOMACH BLEEDING, IT WAS THESE MEDICINES I THINK THAT GOT HIS STOMACH TO THE RAW STATE TO LONG.

WARTS ON FEET

WHAT DO YOU THINK WHEN ONE DAY YOU DON'T HAVE A WART AND IN ONLY FEW DAYS IT THE SIZE OF A 1/2 DOLLAR OR DOLLAR PIECE.

WITHIN A MONTH THIS NOT ONLY GREW FAST, BUT WAS ON THE BOTTOM OF MY FEET.

I ASK THE DOCTOR LATER TO BURN OFF HE SAID THEY WERE TO BIG, AND TOLD BE TO USE OVER COUNTER STUFF, I TRYED WART AWAY, THE SMELL WAS BAD AND DIDN'T HELP. TRYED TO FREEZE THEM OFF THE SMALLER ONE SEEM TO GO AWAY NOT THE BIG ONE. EVEN SHAVED THE BIG ONE OFTEN BUT STOPPED. TRYED PULLING OUT BY THE ROOTS GOT THE SMALLER BUT THE BIG ONE WAS STILL THERE. THIS DID GO AWAY ALMOST LIKE IT CAME.

ONE DAY I NOTICED THEY WERE ALL GONE. THIS WAS ALSO AFTER I HAD GOTTEN OFF OF ALL THE CHOLESTEROL MEDICINE. THEY SO FAR HAVE NOT COME BACK, AS OF NOW. YOU TELL ME, WAS IT THE MEDICINE HELPING THIS GROW? I SAY HELL YES.

I HAD ALSO TALKED TO OTHER PEOPLE WHO TOLD ME THEY HAD A SIMULAR THING HAPPEN. ONE OF THE GUYS I TALKED TO TOLD ME HE WAS HEALTHY, STARTED TAKING THE CHOLESTEROL / STATIN DRUGS AND HE NOTICED WARTS NOT THINKING WAS THE MEDS. HE HAD HIS BURNT OFF LATER, NEXT TIME I SAW HIM, HE ENDED UP HAVING DIABETES AND CANCER. WAS THIS THE MEDS, SOUNDS LIKE IT TO ME. I AM NOT A DOCTOR, BUT I HAVE TALKED TO OVER 600 PEOPLE WHILE IN THE DOCTORS OFFICE OR IN THE HOSPITAL AND ITS

EASY FOR SOMEONE TO START TELLING YOU THERE MEDICAL HISTORY, A HEALTHY PERSON, START TAKING MEDS AND SICK ALL THE TIME. THE COMMON MEDICINE, YOU GUESSED, CHOLESTEROL MEDS. AND THE SIDE AFFECTS PUT THEM ON OTHER MEDS JUST LIKE ME. MOST HAD ALMOST THE SAME MEDS AS I DID. I HAVE A FEW FAMILY MEMBERS WHO TOOK THE CHOLESTEROL MEDICINE AND NOW THERE DIABETIC. WHEN I WAS ON THE FIRST ONE, MY SUGAR LEVELS WHERE GOING CRAZY, MY LEVELS SEEM TO DROP. BUT THIS MEDICINE DID MESS WITH MY SYSTEM. <u>THATS A FACT!</u>

I WANT TO NOTE, AFTER MY RESEARCH ON THESE MEDS, I DID FIND OUT THAT SOME PEOPLE HAD THE SAME THING HAPPEN, AND WAS BELIEVED TO BE FROM ANTI ACIDS, WELL THE CHOLESTEROL MEDICINES PUT ME ON THOSE, SO ITS STILL FROM TAKING THESE MEDS, THIS IS WHAT I SEE AND LIVED THROUGH, SO FAR.

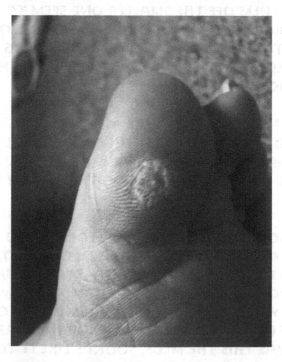

Foot while on meds

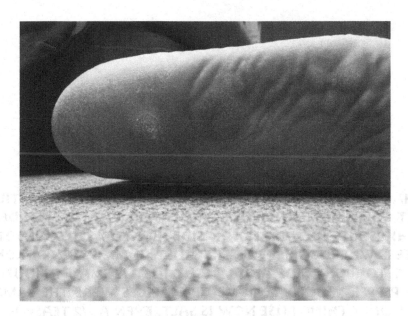

Warts on foot on meds

Foot off meds

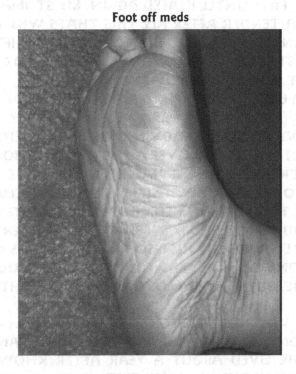

PAINS
(AT RANDOM)

I HAD SOME PAINS THAT WOULD COME AT RANDOM, STILL GET SOME, SOME IN SPOTS WHERE YOU WOULD WONDER WHY IS MY TOE ACHING OR SIDE, BOTTOM OF MY FOOT. THESE WHERE SOME, BUT THE MOST COMMON WAS FROM LEFT TO RIGHT SIDE AND MY GUT JUST A SMALL AMOUNT OF PEPPER WOULD TEAR ME UP & SPICES WERE THE SAME. THE ONLY THING I USE NOW IS SALT. EVEN A 1/2 TEASPOON OF PEPPER I WOULD HURT FOR DAYS AND HAVE TO TAKE MY ANTI ACID PILLS UNTLL HEALED AGAIN. MY STOMACH / GUT AREA IS TO TENDER AFTER ALL THIS THATS WHY I WORRY ABOUT CANCER. I'VE HEARD DOCTORS SAY IF SOMETHING IN THE BODY STAYS RAW TO LONG, IT CAN TURN TO CANCER. I STILL HURT HERE TODAY NOV.23,2011
I'VE HAD A ULCER SO BAD I HAD BLACK STOOLS.

MY STEP DAD & UNCLE HAD AN ULCER BOTH BEFORE THEY DIED. BOTH WHERE BAD. EVERY ONE I HEARD ABOUT THAT HAD PANCREATIC CANCER HAD BEEN ON SOME KIND OF MEDICINE OR SOME KIND OF SICKNESS THAT INCLUDED THE STOMACH. THE COMMON MEDICINE WAS CHOLESTEROL MEDS AND BLOOD THINNERS. MY STEPDAD HAD A ULCER THE SIZE OF A SMALL SAUCER, IT JUST SO HAPPEN HE WAS ON BOTH MEDS AT ONE TIME. HE WAS TREATED FOR THE ULCER AND SENT HOME. BUT STARTED LOSTING WEIGHT RIGHT AFTER.

MY UNCLE WAS HURTING FOR SOME TIME AND WHEN TEST WHERE DONE HE WAS TOLD WHAT HE HAD, PANCREATIC CANCER. HE LIVED ABOUT A YEAR AFTER KNOWING. MY STEPDAD TURNED YELLOW, HAD TEST DONE AND DIED ABOUT

A MONTH LATER. JANUARY 30, 2010. MY UNCLE WAS ON CHOLESTEROL MEDICINE AND MY STEPDAD HAD A DOUBLE WHAMMIE, HE HAD BEEN ON CHOLESTEROL MEDS AND WAS ON OTHERS, ONE WAS A BLOOD THINNER, THE DOCTOR HAD TO TAKE OFF. MY DAD ALSO WAS ON BLOOD THINNERS BEFORE HE DIED, HE ALWAYS COMPLAINED OF STOMACH TROUBLE. ONE OF MY DADS DOCTORS HAD TAKEN HIM OFF OF A LOT OF MEDICINES BECAUSE OF THE SIDE AFFECT THING. ONE PUTTING YOU ON ANOTHER AND ANOTHER, AFTER THIS HE FELT REALY GOOD. BUT AFTER THAT DOCTOR DIED, HE WAS PUT BACK ON SOME OF THE SAME MEDS. HIS HEALTH DROPPED DOWN UNTIL HE DIED. AS OF TODAY MY PAIN IS MOSTLY IN KNEE JOINTS. LEFT THE WORSE, THEN RIGHT AND HIP LAST. WHEN ALL HIT AT ONE TIME CAN'T HARDLY WALK. I HAVE IN MY RIGHT HAND HAD ACHES WHERE THEY ARE HURTING NO MATER WHAT, LATELY HURTING LITE. WHEN ON THE MEDS, ALL THE TIME, DON'T KNOW WHICH ONE WAS CAUSING THIS, BUT ONE OF THE SHEETS OF SIDE AFFECTS I REMEMBER SEEING, OF COARSE THIS WAS LATER, AND TO LATE. WHEN ALL THESE START HITTING YOU AT THE RIGHT TIME ALL TOGETHER, THIS AFFECTS YOUR WORK & MENTAL STATE, EVEN NOW WHILE WRITING THIS BOOK I GET FLARE UPS. SOMETIMES WHEN WRITING BY HAND AND SOME WHILE TYPING. AND ITS NOT FROM THIS IF HURTING BEFORE I START.

I STILL HURT IN MY GUTS FROM TIME TO TIME FRONT CENTER, ONE OF MY DOCTORS TOLD ME I HAD FIBROMYALGIA, THIS IS SOMETHING THAT MAKES YOU HURT ALL OVER AT CERTAIN POINTS, I ACHE AND HURT ALL OVER ALL THE TIME. AGAIN THIS STARTED AFTER TAKING MEDICINES.

PROSCESSED FOOD & MORE

AFTER I NOTICED CHANGES IN MY BODY, ONE OF THE CHANGES IS FOODS I EAT OR DRINK. I NOTICED I WOULD NOT FEEL RIGHT BUT DIDN'T KNOW WHAT WAS GOING ON, SOME TIMES I WOULD GO FOR LONG TIMES FEELING GOOD. THEN I WOULD EAT OR DRINK SOMETHING AND NOTICE SAME CHANGES.

I STOPPED EATING THAT FOOD WHEN I NOTICED MY BRAIN FELT LIKE ELECTRIC CHARGES, MSG? I WAS TOLD THIS MIGHT BE WHAT IS MESSING WITH ME WHEN I WOULD EAT CHINSEE FOOD. I STOPPED EATING DIDN'T HAVE AS MUCH. LATER NOTICED CERTAIN FOODS, LIKE THE MAJOR BRAND H FOODS, THEY ARE GOOD BUT THEY ARE MESSING WITH ME. I WOULD STOP EATING CERTAIN ONES AND NOTICED, AGAIN FOODS I EAT. WOULD CHANGE MY MOODS. I ALSO WENT TO ORGANIC MILK, FILTER MY WATER.

THE TOWN WHERE I LIVE SENT OUT LETTERS WATER NOT GOOD TO DRINK, THIS SEEMED OFTEN AT ONE TIME. I HAD BOUGHT A WATER TEST KIT AND TESTED MYSELF. AT THE TIME I TESTED I FOUND OUT THE WAS WATER HIGH IN PH & ACIDITY, AND AT DANGEROUS LEVELS ACORDING TO MY TEST PACK. THE WATER SMELLS LIKE MUD TO ME, SOMETIMES BLEACH. I FEEL STICKY WHEN I BATHE, YOU CAN'T BLAME THE TOWN IF, THE WATER FORMULA WAS CHANGED BY THE GOVERMENT. THIS CHANGE I NOTICED AND MANY OTHERS. WHAT WAS WRONG WITH THE OLD FORMULA? WAS NEVER TOLD.

WAS TOLD YESTERDAY BY A WORKER IN TOWN, THE WATER TODAY HAS A COMPUTER TO MIX THE CHEMICALS, ALL DONE BY MACHINE, SO IF YOU DON'T HAVE COMPUTER TROUBLE

YOUR O.K., BUT BE REAL, WHO DOES'T, AND HOW WILL YOU KNOW WHEN THIS GOES BAD, WHEN ITS TO LATE? I FOUND OUT THAT ONE OF THE MEDS I WAS ON CAN CAUSE THESE ALLERGIC REACTIONS AND MORE.

WHILE TYPING THIS BOOK MY COMPUTER WENT OUT ABOUT 3 TIMES, I GOT A FRIEND AND OWNER OF TRANSECH TO PATCH UP AND THE LAST TIME HAD TO BUY A NEW COMPUTER TO FINISH, UNLESS I AM DIEING, I DO NOT WANT MY LIFE TO DEPEND <u>ON ANY COMPUTER.</u>

DRUG-6

ST-STUDERD & FACE CHANGES?

WHILE ON ANOTHER STOMACH MED I SEEM TO START STUDDERING, I SHOULD SAY I NOW KNOW IT WAS THE RG-BRAND, I WAS HAVING TROUBLE AND DID NOT KNOW WHAT OR WHICH MEDICINE WAS CAUSING.

MY FACE WOULD HAVE WEIRD TWITCHING, AND I WOULD STUDDER, I'AM SURE THIS IS WHEN I WAS ON THE BRAND-RG. (NOTE THE PICTURE OF NERVES IN HEAD AND THE ONE I DREW) IF I REMEMBER THE RG-BRAND WAS TO HELP MY STOMACH BUT I WAS GETTING SICKER ON THIS AND LATER STOPPED. I WAS ALSO GIVEN THIS FOR SOME TEST I TOOK AT THE HOSPITAL BUT NEVER REALY NOTICED I HAD TAKEN BEFORE AND HAD TROUBLE, JUST REMEMBER TAKING BEFORE, SO I TOOK THIS MED AGAIN, WHEN I TOOK THE COLON TEST. I LATER NOTICE SOME OF THE OLD TROUBLES HAD COME BACK THE LAST TIME I WAS TO TAKE THE SAME TEST I TOLD THE HOSPITAL I COULD'NT TAKE. SO THEY SAID DON'T WORRY. THIS WAS AROUND JUNE 2010. I REMEMBER RG WAS THE DRUG I TOOK WHEN WORKING ON THE BOAT, A NEW JOB AND HAD TO QUIT. 150.00 A DAY. FROM ABOUT 35.00 A DAY THIS IS WHY THE MENTAL STRESS OF THE WHOLE THING WAS SO BAD. MORE OF THIS IN ANOTHER PART OF THIS BOOK.

I WAS ALSO HAVING WEARD MUSCLE CONTRACTIONS, YOU COULD WATCH MY STOMACH MOVE AND JUMP LIKE SOMETHING WAS INSIDE WANTING TO PUSH OUT OR KICKING OUT. AFTER READING THE SIDE AFFECTS I UNDERSTOOD

WHICH MEDICINES WHERE DOING WHAT TO ME, IN SOME CASES THEY ALL DONE THE SAME THING, THIS DRUG SAID IT MADE THE STOMACH WORK FASTER TO GET THE FOOD OUT BEFORE THE BODY COULD TAKE IN THE CHOLESTEROL, BUT THIS ALSO GIVE ME THE STOMACH TROUBLE I TALKED ABOUT. THIS DRUG WAS ON TV JUST AFTER I GOT SICK FOR GIVING PEOPLE SOME OF THESE SAME TROUBLES, LIP SMACKING AND MORE, AND I STILL HAVE SOME OF THESE TROUBLES.

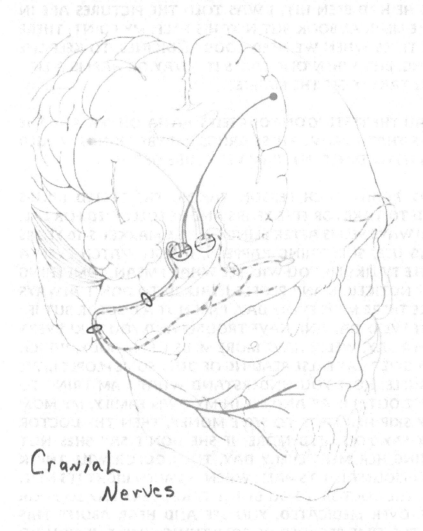

Cranial
Nerves

MEDICINES YOU HAVE TO TAKE RISK FOR

THERE ARE MEDICINES I WOULD TAKE IF I HAD TO. ONE OF MY FAMILY MEMBERS HAD A KIDNEY TRANSPLANT, HE HAS TO TAKE MEDICINE FOR LIFE. HE HAS HIS UPS AND DOWNS BUT IS DOING GOOD. ONE TIME HE HAD TROUBLE WITH SOME MEDICINES, BUT THE DOCTORS IN NEW ORLEANS GOT ON THIS RIGHT AWAY AND FIXED THIS, HE WAS BUSING LIKE HE HAD BEEN HIT, I WAS TOLD THE PICTURES ARE IN SOME MEDICAL BOOK BUT NOT HIS FACE. MY POINT, THERE ARE TIMES WHEN WE NEED GOOD MEDICINES, TO KEEP LIFE GOING, BUT WHEN ONE TAKES IT AWAY OR HARMS A LIFE, WELL TAKE IT OFF THE MARKET.

DO ALL THE TESTING ON YOURSELFS. HA HA. OH YEA, AND THE ONES THAT APROVE THESE DRUGS. MAYBE THINGS WOULD BE A LITTLE DIFFERENT, I'AM VERY SURE OF THAT.

I SAY AGAIN, EACH PERSON TAKING THE TESTED DRUGS NEED TO TAKE FOR FIVE YEARS AND BE FOLLOWED FOR LIFE. IT ALWAYS SEEMS AFTER BEING ON THE MARKET 5-10 YEARS LONG USE, SOMETHING HAPPENS, IF YOU WATCH EVEN A LITTLE TV LIKE ME YOU WILL SEE WHAT I MEAN. SOMETHING ESE I NOTICED. MANY PEOPLE I TALKED TO DON'T ALWAYS TAKE THERE MEDS EVERY DAY, I AM NOT A DOCTOR BUT IF I TAKE EVERY DAY AND HAVE TROUBLE AND YOU TAKE EVERY OTHER DAY, WELL I HAVE MORE MEDS IN MY BODY, WHICH MAY GIVE THAT FALSE READING OF ONLY SOME PEOPLE HAVE TROUBLE, HOPE YOU UNDERSTAND WHAT I AM TRING TO POINT OUT. I HEAR AND SEE IN MY OWN FAMILY, MY MOM MAY SKIP HER MEDS TO SAVE MONEY, THEN THE DOCTOR MAY SAY YOU NEED MORE, IF SHE DON'T SAY SHES NOT TAKING HER MEDS EVERY DAY, THE DOCTOR WILL THINK THE AMOUNT IS TO SMALL, WHEN IF TAKEN RIGHT ITS NOT. TELL THE DOCTOR IF YOU DON'T TAKE EVERY DAY SO YOUR NOT OVER MEDICATED, YOU SEE AND HEAR ABOUT THIS ALL THE TIME BECAUSE OF SOMETHING SIMPLE. IF YOU DO TAKE MEDS ON REGULAR BASIS, THEN THE DOCTOR WILL

HAVE TO DEPEND ON YOU TO TELL HIM IF YOU THINK YOUR OVER OR UNDER MEDICATED, BY THE WAY YOU FEEL. I SEE MANY FAMILY MEMBERS THAT HAVE MEDICINE RAISED AND LOWERED EVERY FEW MONTHS.

NEVER TELL THEM OR YOU GO TO JAIL, YOU ALWAYS THINK YOUR OVER OR UNDER A LOCATION, ITS THE WAY YOU FEEL. THE MANY MANY MONTHS THAT THEY PUT MEDICINE RAN, OFF AND ON FOR SEVERAL MONTHS.

WHAT IT FEELS LIKE?

IT WAS LIKE LOSING YOUR LIFE FOR 5+ YEARS, YOU CAN'T DO ANYTHING WHEN YOUR WORRIED ABOUT WHATS GOING ON, SICK ONE DAY, FEEL GOOD THE NEXT5 MINUTES LATER WANT TO GO TO THE HOSPITAL. ITS A NIGHTMARE!!! I DIDN'T WANT TO TRAVEL OUT OF TOWN TO FLA. TO SEE MY AUNT BECAUSE I WAS WORRYED ABOUT HAVING A PANIC ATTACK ON THE ROAD OR HEART ATTACK THIS IS WHAT I THOUGHT I WAS HAVING ALL THE TIME. EVEN OUT OF TOWN WITH FAMILY OR FRIENDS IS A NIGHTMARE, YOUR ON THE ROAD NEVER KNOW IF YOUR HAVING A HEART ATTACK, YOUR AWAY FROM A DOCTOR OR HOSPITAL, YOU JUST FREAK OUT SOMETIMES, YOU JUST DON'T WANT TO TELL THEM WHY. WE DID STILL GO AND I HAD TO KEEP A WET COLD RAG AROUND, BROKE OUT IN A SWEAT AT ONE TIME. WANTED THE AIR ON ME AT ALL TIMES, COLD AS I COULD GET. MY STEPDAD WAS COLD SO THERE WERE TIMES I JUST HAD TO TURN DOWN THE AC. I'VE WHEN OUT OF TOWN WITH FRIENDS AND ITS A NIGHTMARE, YOUR AT THERE MERCY IF YOU DON'T FEEL RIGHT, I KEPT THE AC IN MY FACE, THIS TENDS TO HELP. THEY WANT TO TALK AND YOU ARE NERVOUS AND WANT TO CLOSE YOUR EYES AND TRY TO SLEEP OFF, FEW TIMES WE STOP FOR GAS I GOT A COLD BOTTLE OF WATER AND PAPER TOWEL, THEN WOULD PUT ON FACE. THIS DOESN'T HAPPEN AS MUCH ANY MORE, BUT THIS DOES STILL HAPPEN. I TRY TO KEEP MY PILLS IN EASY REACH, MY BOSS TOLD ME I HAVE IN EVERY CAR, I ASKED HOW HE KNEW. HE WAS JUST MAKING FUN, AND SAID HE REALY DIDN'T KNOW BUT LAUGHED WHEN I TOLD HIM IT WAS TRUE. I TEND TO KEEP AT LEAST 3 PILLS AT ANYTIME IN ONE OF MY CARS AND WORK, JUST IN CASE. WHEN BEING STOPPED BY THE POLICE, THIS WAS GREAT WHEN HAVING AN ANXIETY ATTACK, ONE COP ASKED WHY

I WAS SO NERVOUS. I FLAT OUT SAID TO HIM, YOU HAD NO REASON FOR STOPPING ME HE SAID I DID'NT HAVE MY SEAT BELTS ON, I TOLD HIM I DIDN'T BELIEVE IN WEARING ALL THE TIME BECAUSE I AM . . . ALIVE TODAY BECAUSE I DIDN'T WEAR A FEW TIMES. SOMETHING SAID DON'T WEAR, GOD? I BELIEVE IN GOD, DON'T PUSH MY THOUGHTS ON ANY ONE UNLESS ASKED, MY BELIEFS MADE ME NOT WANT TO PUT MY SEAT BELTS ON, AND THIS SAVED MY LIFE. NOT THE GOVERMENT LAWS. WHICH BY THE WAY IF I DIE BECAUSE I HAD TO WEAR A SEAT BELT, THEN THAT MAKES THE STATE A MURDER. THINK OF IT, IF I FORCE SOMEONE TO DO SOMETHING, I'AM IN TROUBLE FOR IT. WHY NOT THEM. THEY SHOULD PAY THE FUNERAL COST, AND GIVE MONEY TO THE FAMILYS. I GOT IN A WRECK AND THE SEAT BELT WAS PULLED INTO THE SEAT, I WOULD HAVE BEEN CUT INTO. AND AT ABOUT 17 YEARS OLD, 54 THIS MONTH, AND WRITING ABOUT THE PAST. THE BEST THING IS I WOULD NOT START MY CAR OR LET ANY ONE AT THAT TIME RIDE WITHOUT WEARING BELTS AND I ALSO SENT A LETTER TO THE STATE. ASKING FOR A LAW PASSED. THIS WAS THE 70S. I WAS TOLD THIS VIOLATED RELIGIOUS RIGHTS.

WELL NOW I KNOW IT DOES!!!! MINE.
 WEAR A SEAT BELT? I'VE SEEN MANY WRECKS AND HAVE SEEN IN FRONT OF ME, I'AM ALWAYS FEW SECONDS BEHIND, OR HAPPENS AFTER I PASS. WHY?? I KNOW. BUT THIS IS ANOTHER BOOK I WILL WORK ON. MY BELIEF IN GOD. I COULD TELL YOU THINGS THAT WOULD CURL YOUR HAIR OF WHAT HAPPENED TO ME.

ITS EVERY DAY THINGS LIKE THIS THAT WERE SO BAD, NOT KNOWING HOW YOU WOULD FEEL IN A PROBLEM LIKE WHAT YOU JUST READ, I JUST TRY TO RELAX AS SOON AS I GET HOME, KINDA NAP IT OFF. IT HELPED SOMETIMES, OTHER TIMES, DIDN'T WORK. THATS WHEN I WOULD GO TO WORK WITH SOMETHING ON MY MIND, LIKE THIS, AND IT AFFECTS YOUR WORK, YOU FORGET THINGS OR, ONE TIME I HAD PUT A MOVIE TOGETHER BACKWARDS! YES THE KIDS MUST HAVE

THOUGHT WAS FUNNY BUT NOT MY BOSS. I WAS LET GO FOR ABOUT A WEEK, I WAS'NT THERE WHEN THE MOVIE RAN, I HAD GOT IT READY FOR THE KIDS AND MY BOSS HAD TO JUST PRESS A BUTTON, BUT WHEN THE END OF THE MOVIE COME ON FIRST, I AM SURE I WAS CUSTED OUT TO THE LOWEST. HAD I BEEN THERE I COULD HAVE MADE SOME CHANGES AND STILL RUN, NOT LIKE NORMAL BUT WOULD HAVE WORKED.

BUT I WAS HOME FOR SOME REASON. ANYWAY, THE TROUBLES DISRUPT YOUR LIFE HORRIBLY.

YES, I'AM STILL THERE, EVEN AFTER ALL THAT.

I WANT TO NOTE SOMETHING, I ALSO ASKED MY FAMILY IF I DO DIE IN A WRECK AND THEY SAY IT WAS BECAUSE OF A SEATBELT TO FILE A CLAIM AGINST THE STATE.

HOW I FEEL NOW

I AM WEAK 98% OF THE TIME, I ACHE ALMOST EVERY DAY, JOINTS RIGHT LEG AND HIP ON RIGHT SIDE. MY LEFT KNEE HURTS AT THIS TIME OF WRITING, I HAD A WEAK SPELL AND HURT BY LANDING ON MY LEFT SIDE. ITS IN THE BOOK ALSO I AM SURE YOU READ BY NOW, EVERY DAY A NEW ADVENTURE. MY HEAD BOTHERS ME SOMETIMES FEELS LIKE WHEN I DON'T TAKE MY BLOOD PRESURE MEDS. ONE BRAND OF MED I WAS ON I DON'T EVER REMEMBER HAVING A HEADACHE. I ALSO FELT GOOD UNTILL THESE MEDS IN THE BOOK CHANGED MY LIFE. I STILL TAKE THE NERVE PILL I CALL IT, MY BRAND—5 BUT ONLY WHEN NEEDED TRY NEVER TO TAKE FOR MORE THAN ONE DAY—TWO MAX. I'AM WEAK ALL THE TIME, WANT TO NAP A LOT. FEEL DRAINED SO I TAKE A NAP, WAKE UP RE-FRESHED, BUT ONLY LAST FEW HOURS AND DRAINED AGAIN.

<u>MYASTHENIA GRAVIS</u>—THIS IS A NEUROMUSCULAR DISORDER VARIABLE WEAKNESS OF VOLUNTARY MUSCLES, WHICH OFTEN IMPROVE WITH REST AND WHEN ACTIVE WORSENS. THIS WAS SAID TO BE A SIDE AFFECT OF ONE OF THE MEDICINES I WAS ON. NOTE: NO DOCTOR SAID I HAVE OR HAD THIS, BUT THIS IS ABOUT THE CLOSEST THING TO ALL OF MY COMPAINTS OF WHATS GOING ON WITH ME. DO I HAVE, DON'T KNOW BUT WHEN I SAW THIS MY JAW DROPPED, AND <u>THERE IS NO KNOWN CURE FOR THIS</u>. LOOK IT UP. THERES A LOT OF THINGS LISTED I HAVE, OR HAD.

ALWAYS HAVE TROUBLE CRAPPING, TRY TO EAT RASIN BRAND OR SHREDDED WHEAT THIS HELPS MOST ALL THE TIME BUT NOT ALL THE TIME, I NEVER HAD TROUBLE LIKE THIS UNTILL I STARTED THESE MEDICINES, FACT! I LIKE SUGAR ON MINE

AND SOMETIMES I GAIN A LITTLE WEIGHT BACK BECAUSE I HAVE TROUBLE WALKING. I HAD 8 ACRES OF LAND, BUT SOLD SOME BECAUSE NEEDED MONEY FOR WHAT EVER AT THAT TIME. SOMETIMES AS YOU READ I HAD TO TAKE OFF OF WORK. MONEY GOT TO COME FROM SOME WHERE, EVERY ONE KNOWS DON'T SELL LAND GOES UP IN VALUE, THIS MEDICINE COST ME THAT. LAND MY DAD HAD IS WHAT I SOLD I WANTED TO KEEP IT IN THE FAMILY, I DID RENT SOME OF IT LATER, THIS IS WHAT HELPS ME NOW. I HAVE BEEN KEEPING TRACK OF HOW I FEEL BECAUSE IF SOMETHING HAPPENS I HAVE A RECORD OF WHAT HAPPENED. ITS NOT NORMAL TO HAVE TROUBLE THATS FROM DRUGS, AND ONCE YOU GET OFF YOUR TROUBLES SHOULD GO AWAY. ONE DOCTOR TOLD ME MEDICINE GETS IN YOUR FAT CELLS AND CAN STAY FOR UP TO A YEAR OR MORE, SOME DRUGS ARE CONCIDERED TOXIC AND ACUMULATE AND NEVER LEAVE. MY CHOLESTEROL LEVELS STILL STAY AROUND 190-230 AS FAR AS I KNOW. THIS IS WHAT ONE DOCTOR SAYS DON'T GET BELOW 200. IF ITS NOT A LIFE SAVING DRUG I WILL NOT TAKE. I DO NOT NEED MORE DRUG HORROR IN MY LIFE. I'AM 54 AT THIS TIME AND LOST ABOUT 5 YEARS OF MY LIFE TO THIS AND WILL SUFFER THE REST FROM THIS MESS, WELL IT SEEMS THAT WAY. AND SO FAR I HAVEN'T BEEN WRONG.

I NOTICED WHEN TAKING THE ACID REDUCER XX THE ONLY DRUG THAT HELPED IN A GOOD WAY, BUT WEAKNESS WAS ANOTHER SIDE AFFECT, AND SOME NOT LISTED HERE. IF OVER THE COUNTER DRUGS FOR ANTI ACID WAS USED WITH THIS I HAD WROKE UP WITH BLOOD IN MY EYES, DON'T KNOW IF THAT HURT MY EYES YET.

THE OVER THE COUNTER CRANBERRY PILLS SAY TO HELP CLEAN YOUR BLADDER, AND URINE TRACK. I GOT DIZZY WHEN I TOOK, DON'T KNOW LONG TERM AFFECT OF THAT EITHER. STATIN DRUGS AND OTHER CHOLESTEROL MEDICINES WHERE THE REASON I TOOK THIS AND OTHER THINGS FOR MY STOMACH. I WAS HURTING SO BAD ONE TIME I JUST KNEW I WAS GOING TO DIE SOON. I HAD A FRIEND DIE, HIS STOMACH

WAS HURTING THEY RUSHED HIM TO THE HOSPITAL, HE DIED ON THE TABLE, I WAS TOLD HE DIDN'T TAKE HIS MEDS THAT MUCH BUT THAT HOSPITAL HAS A BAD REP. ANOTHER BOOK I GUESS, WELL HERE'S A SHORT ONE. I WENT THERE AFTER BLEEDING IN MY THROAT I TRYED TO SWALLOW SOMETHING AND COULDN'T. I WAS LATER TOLD I COULD HAVE DIED, BECAUSE THEY DIDN'T TAKE ANY TEST TO SEE IF I TORE MY GUT INSIDE. THIS IS ONE OF MANY HORRORS ALSO IN MY LIFE AND FAMILY OR FRIENDS. THIS IS ALSO A SIDE AFFECT OF ONE OF THE MEDS I WAS ON, THE MUSCLES IN THE THROAT ARE RELAXED AND MAKES IT HARD TO SWALLOW. THIS ALSO CAUSES ACID RE-FLUX, WHICH I'VE BEEN TOLD MANY TIMES I HAD. BUT OFF THE MEDICINES AND KNOWING WHAT FOODS THAT GIVE ME TROUBLE, I DON'T HAVE AS MUCH TROUBLE NOW. I DO TRY TO STAY AWAY FROM ANYTHING THAT GIVES ME SOUR STOMACH. IF I HAVE TROUBLE, TAKE OVER THE COUNTER STUFF, SEEMS TO HELP A LOT.

I ALSO FEEL LIKE I CAN'T TRUST ANYONE WHEN I ASK FOR HELP AND DON'T GET, YOU'RE HURTING ASK FOR TEST THAT THE DOCTOR SHOULD BE WANTING. THIS TOOK MY FINANCES AND JUST TRYED TO GET A LOAN AT LOCAL BANK BEEN DEALING WITH FOR YEARS. NO LOAN, THE REASON, TO MANY MEDICAL COLECTIONS, AND THESE ARE OF WHEN I WENT TO DOCTORS OR EMERGENCY HOSPITALS THAT WHERE OUT OF MY CONTROL. IT WAS GO TO HOSPITAL OR DIE, AFTER ALL I DON'T KNOW WHATS GOING ON, I HAD TO LEARN, EVERY LITTLE TROUBLE IS THIS REAL OR JUST MEDICINES MAKING MY HEART RACE. IS IT RACEING BECAUSE I NEED TO SEE A DOCTOR, HOPE YOU GET THE PICTURE, YOUR IN A STATE OF SHOCK YOU DON'T KNOW WHATS GOING ON YOUR AT THE MERCY OF SOMEONE ESE, AND THEN SOME WILL SAY WELL YOU HAD AN ANXIETY ATTACK, BUT AT THE SAME TIME SAY GOOD THING YOU CAME IN, IT COULD HAVE BEEN A HEART ATTACK. AGAIN THE HORROR OF NOT KNOWING, THE PAIN OF THE OTHER TROUBLES AND STRESS. I THINK I SAID THIS BEFORE, THE MENTAL HORROR, IS THIS MY TIME TO DIE. EVERY TIME I HAVE BREATHING TROUBLE STILL

TODAY I WONDER HOW LONG BEFORE IT GETS WORSE OR IS ALL THIS MESS LEVELED TO A POINT WHERE I CAN SAY, I'AM NOT HEALED BUT CAN LIVE WITH NO MORE HORROR IN MY LIFE. LIKE I SAID BEFORE EVERYDAY HAS A NEW NIGHTMARE JUST LERKING WAITING TO JUMP OUT AT ME, OR IF YOUR STILL ON THESE MEDICINES, <u>YOU!!!</u>

I'VE HAD HIGH ANXIETY ATTACKS JUST THINKING AND WORRYING WILL THIS TROUBLE HIT ME WHEN I'AM IN A CAR DRIVING ON THE HWY, IN A LONG LINE AT CHECK OUT, CHURCH, AT WORK, AND OTHER PLACES. I WANT YOU TO THINK IF THIS HAPPENED TO ME WOULD YOU WANT TO BE AWAY FROM SOMEONE WHO CAN HELP YOU IF THIS WAS A REAL HEART ATTACK, YOUR HAVING TROUBLE BREATHING AND YOU START TO PANIC YOUR ON A HWY, YOUR 30 MILES FROM ANYTHING, AND NO ONE IS ON THE ROAD BUT YOU. PLEASE COOL DOWN THIS WAS ONLY A TEST, GET THE POINT. I HARDLY HAVE NOW BUT WAS A NIGHTMARE WHEN I WAS ON THESE MEDICINES.

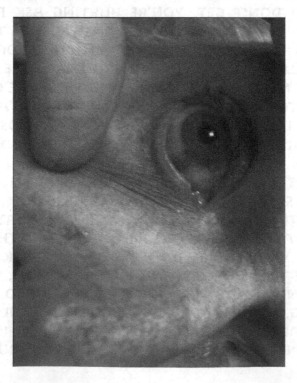

80

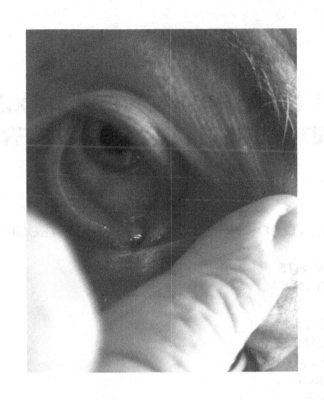

LIST OF ALMOST EVERY TROUBLE I HAD & SOME I STILL HAVE FROM ALL THE MEDS I TOOK

GOT TIME TO READ?   * = I STILL HAVE TROUBLE WITH

COLD SWEATS
CONFUSION
BLURRY VISION
HEADACHES *
NERVOUSNESS **
RAPID HEART RATE *
TREMBLING *
DIZZINESS
MEMORY TROUBLE **
MUSCLE PAIN **
POUNDING HEARTBEAT SENSATIONS *
SLEEPING DIFFICULTY **

HOT COLD FLASHES
ABNORMAL URINE / BLOOD IN URINE */ DARK
MUSCLE STIFFNESS *
ALLERGIC REACTIONS TO OTHER MEDS, FOODS, DYES, AND
PRESERVATIVES ***
LITE FEVER & TIREDNESS *
JOINT PAINS *************** * *
BLISTERING, PEELING SKIN
YELLOW EYES * & SKIN
CONSTIPATION ALLTHE TIME *   *   *
HEART BURN *
STOMACH GAS, PAIN, UPSET *

SWELLING OF RESPIRATORY ORGANS
DIFFICULTY IN BREATHING *
BLOATING-NAUSEA *
ITCHING
TIGHTNESS IN THE CHEST *
BONE PAIN *
TENDON PAIN
PERSISTENT SORE THROAT
PAINFUL URINATION
SEVERE PAIN IN THE STOMACH *******
ANKLES SWELLING

PANCREATITIS
RAISED RED RASH
TINGLING SENSATION & NUMBNESS
DEPRESSION ******************
STUFFY NOISE, COLD SYMPTOMS
BACK PAIN
COUGH
STOMACH ULCER ******************
ELEVATED BLOOD SUGAR LEVELS

INVOLUNTARY MOVEMENTS
IMPAIRED FINGER MOVEMENTS
TREMORS / PARKINSON LIKE SYMPTOMS
ANXIETY ******
RESTLESS LEG SYSDROME
MUSCLE SPASMS***
NUMBNESS IN THE FACE
TROUBLE SWALLOWING-LIKE MUSCLES STOPPED
SLURRED SPEECH-MUMBLING *
DROOLING SALIVA
  FIBROMYALGIA **
        PAIN ALL OVER BODY
        LIKE PINS & NEEDLES
        SHOULDER PAIN-HIP, KNEE
        FEET
COPD *

SHORT OF BREATH*—BOUTS OF BRONCHITIS

HIGH CK-LEVELS
START OF A CATARACT
LIGHT HEADEDNESS
MUSCLE TWITCHING
STAMMERING-STUTTERING **
SUICIDAL THOUGHTS
TROUBLE SPEAKING **
NASAL CONGESTION ******
ACID REFLUX ********
DROWSINESS**
IRREGULAR HEARTBEAT*
SKIN CANCER
WARTS—GONE AFTER OF MEDS * WEARD RIGHT*
    * * * DIFFICULTY—CLIMBING STAIRS * * *
              LIFTING OBJECTS
   NEED HANDS TO RISE FROM SITTING, MOST OF TIME

I'LL STOP HERE YOU'RE TIRED, I AM SURE.

MAYBE FEW MORE

PERSISTENT SORE THROAT
HARD SWALLOWING
SWOLLEN THROAT
SWELLING OF TONGUE

    THIS IS SOME I HAD OR STILL HAVE TROUBLE WITH FROM ALL THE DRUGS INCLUDING FINANCIAL TROUBLE AND THESE MEDICINES CAUSED TROUBLE FOR ME AT WORK, TAKING OFF A LOT 1 DAY, 1 WEEK TO OVER A MONTH+ OFF AND HAD TO USE MY SAVINGS MONEY FROM INHERITANCE, IF I WOULDN'T HAVE HAD THIS MONEY I DON'T KNOW WHAT WOULD HAVE HAPPENED, AND THIS WAS A LIVE CHANGING AMOUNT OF MONEY. NOW ITS ALL GONE BUT ABOUT $ 2000.00 AS OF THIS WRITING. I WILL NOT SAY THE AMOUNT BUT WAS LARGE FOR SOMEONE LIKE ME.

NOTES FROM DOCTORS ON MY MEDICAL RECORDS

FROM JULY 17, 2001 TILL—SEPTEMBER 2010 NOT ALL HOSPITAL VISITS ARE INCLUDED BUT SOME ARE MENTIONED I ALSO FORGOT TO SAY THERE WERE MORE HOSPITALS, 5 ALL TOGETHER AND TWO REGULAR DOCTORS AND MANY HOSPITAL DOCTORS SOME ONLY SAW ONCE, SOME I SAW FEW TIMES, THATS SOME HEAVY DUTY DOCTORING

HERE ARE SOME QUICK DATES TO SHOW WHEN SOME OF MY TROUBLES WITH CHOLESTEROL MEDICINE HAPPENED OR ABOUT TIME STARTED, SOME TROUBLES I STILL HAVE.

ON: JULY 17, 2001 SHOWS FIRST VISIT WITH THIS DOCTOR. NOTED NO CHEST PAINS OR PALITATIONS, ALSO GIVEN ONE OF THE FIRST DRUG'S TO CHANGE MY LIFE. DRUG #1 ANTI INFLAMITORY DRUG—NOW OFF MARKET

AUGUST 15, 2001 SHOWS ALREADY COMPLANING OF CHEST DISCOMFORT AND ALSO UPPER GASTRIC PAIN. PAINS ARE SHARP AND AT TIMES DO RADIATE TO BOTH SHOULDERS. I COMPLAINED OF SWALLOWING. NOTED REFLUX DISEASE NOW. AND SCHEDULED FOR A STRESS TEST, ALONG WITH GASTROENTEROLOGIST SERVICE. GIVEN. ACID REDUCEING DRUG

SEPTEMBER 7, 2001 <u>HOSPITAL VISIT</u>—NOTES HAD EKG 2 DAYS AGO, ABDOMINAL PAIN FOR 2-3 MONTHS—NAUSEA—PAIN ON SIDE-GI COCKTALE GIVEN—TOLD—GERD WAS THE ANSWER, PALPATIONS ALSO NOTED

SEPTEMBER 12, 2001 VISIT

DECEMBER 12,2001 SHOWS STARTING TO HAVE TROUBLE SLEEPING, AND HAD BEEN PUT ON MORE MEDICINE. PUT ON DRUG ## AND DRUG## NOTE CAN'T READ OTHER ON LIST.

APRIL 12, 2002 NOW SHOWS ANXIETY-HYPERLIPIDEMIA-HYPERTENSION-ED-GERD—AND PUT ON NEW MEDS. NERVE PILL AND SUPER PILL ALSO NOTE I HAD COMPAINED OF THINKING I MAY HAVE DIABETES AND SKIN CANCER, I NOW HAVE A HISTORY OF PANIC ATTACKS AND HAVE BEEN SEEN IN THE EMERGENCY ROOM. I REMEMBER MY SUGAR GOING UP AND DOWN AND SPOTS ON SKIN. THIS MUST HAVE BEEN ABOUT THE TIME I COMPAINED OF TROBING IN MY NECK. IT NOTES CHECKING MY NECK.

JUNE 12, 2002 **HOSPITAL VISIT**—HEART FLUTERING AND BEATING RAPID TIGHT IN THE CHEST, SHORT OF BREATH, LAB WORK, EKG, CPK,—DIAGNOSIS—PALPITATIONS NOTES 4 MEDS ON, ONE HAS BEEN ON TV FOR HEART ATTACKS AND DEATH!!!! THIS IS ALSO WHEN THEY PUT THE HEART MONITOR FOR A DAY ON ME.

OCTOBER 24, 2002 NOW SHOWS HYPERTENSION—OBESITY—ANXIETY   DISORDER—ED—GERD—AND HYPERLIPIDEMIA. I WAS HAVING BACK PAIN NO TRAUMA. WAS TAKING PAIN PILLS. ALSO SHOWS NOW ON ANTI ACID.

DECEMBER 11, 2002 **HOSPITAL VISIT**—ON MY MOMS BIRTHDAY. NOTES PALITATIONS AGAIN, WENT TO STORE WHERE THERE WAS SMOKING, 15 MIN. LATER HEART BEATING FAST HAD HAPPENED 7 OTHER TIMES NOTED. NOTES MEDS ON AGAIN, ONE ON TV FOR HEART ATTACKS, OX LEVEL 98% BLOOD PRESSURE LOW FOR ME. UNDER 100 /63 ALSO NOTES CARDIOLOGY CONSULTATION

JANUARY 6, 2003 NOW HAVE BEEN COMPAINING OF BLOOD IN URINE. AND HAVE A IVP. SHOWS GROSS HEMATURIA, BLOOD IN MY URINE.

JANUARY 16, 2003 <u>HOSPITAL ACC CLINIC</u>—NOTES ON 4 MEDS ONE ON TV AND ANTI ACID DRUG ALSO. CHECK UP AFTER HOSPITAL VISIT

MARCH 10, 2003 HYPERTENSION—HYPERLIPIDEMIA—ANXIETY DEPRESSION—ED—GERD—AND HISTORY OF GROSS HEMATURIA

APRIL 23, 2003 ON CHOLESTEROL MEDS, AND NOW HAVE NOTED—CHEST BILATERAL COARSE CREPITATIONS, OCCASIONAL WHEEZING. I NOW HAVE ACUTE BRONCHITIS.

JULY 23, 2003 THIS IS ABOUT THE TIME I BECAME MORE SENSITIVE TO GRASS AND OTHER THINGS, NOTES, CUT GRASS AND HAVING TROUBLE. ALSO HAVING SKIN RASHS. GIVEN CREAM AND REFILLED ONE OF MY DRUGS, SHOWS ALL THE ABOVE WITH SKIN RASH ADDED.

SEPTEMBER 12, 2003 <u>HOSPITAL VISIT</u>—PAIN TO SHOULDER NO TRAUMA—HURT FOR 2-3 DAYS AND NOTES ON THE CHOLESTEROL MEDS ALONG WITH THE OTHERS.

SEPTEMBER 15, 2003 NOW SHOWS TAKING <u>ANOTHER ANTI INFLAMITORY DRUG LIKE FIRST ONE</u>, AND TESTERONE LEVEL TEST NOTED.

JANUARY 26, 2004 SHOWS IREGULAR HEARTBEAT AND PAIN IN RIB CAGE I CAN'T MAKE OUT THE OTHER STUFF, BUT THE DOCTOR FILLED THE PAGE WITH WRITING.

FEBRUARY 2, 2004 FOR LAB WORK? DID NOTE A NEW MEDICINE CREAM FOR RASH.

FEBRUARY 24, 2004 <u>HOSPITAL VISIT</u>—SUDDEN ON SET OF DIZZINESS, AND SHORT OF BREATH, NOTES MAY BE AN ALLERGIC REACTION—ALSO NOTES IN MY BEHAVIOR—ANXIOUS, THIS IS MOST LIKELY THE START OF THE WORST TO COME. DON'T KNOW WHY BUT PUTS NAME OF DRUG MAKER ON MY

RECORDS, AND SHOWS JUST YESTERDAY HAD A X-RAY UNDER SPECIAL NOTES THERES 1ST MENTION OF MY BREATHING TEST, AND TO KEEP THE APOINTMENT

MARCH 6, 2004 <u>HOSPITAL VISIT</u>—CONSTIPATION FOR 3 WEEKS, MOST LIKELY FROM THE PAIN PILLS, THEY GIVE ME A ENEMA HAD TO RUN DOWN HALL WITH ONLY A SHEET ON, ZIG ZAG IN HALLWAYS OF THE HOSPITAL TO GO TO THE TOLET, WHAT IF I COULD NOT HAVE MADE IT, WELL THERE WOULD HAVE BEEN A BIG MESS, IT LOOKED LIKE THEY GAVE ME 2 GALLONS OF THAT STUFF THE'RE WERE ALSO TWO NURSES TO GIVE ME AN ENEMA, THIS WAS ONE SUPER HEAVY DUTY ENEMA, HA HA, ALSO NOTED A NEW VERSION OF MEDICINE AGAIN ON TV FOR HEART ATTACKS AND OTHER THINGS, AGE 46 AT THIS TIME. IF I WOULD HAVE LOST MY STEET WHILE RUNNING, RAY STEVENS WOULD HAVE TO UPDATE THE STREAK SONG, "LOOKING FOR THE TOLET" OR THEY CALL ME THE STREAK WITH A BELLY OF FLEET, BUY THE WAY HE'S STILL ALIVE AND SINGING AS OF THIS WRITING.

APRIL 5, 2004 ALL THE ABOVE WITH RIGHT SHOULDER PAIN NOW. ALSO NOTED TO HAVE A GI SERVICE AT LCMC, FOR CHRONIC CONSTIPATION. <u>STILL ON PAIN PILLS</u>. NOTED USE ANTI INFLAMITORY DRUG DAILY AS NEEDED.

MAY 11, 2004 <u>HOSPITAL VISIT</u>—RIGHT SIDE PAIN FOR 2 MONTHS PICKING PAIN AS BAD AS 10 ON THE RATING SCALE-BURNING ON URINANTION—NOTED MAY BE RELATED TO MEDS—ALSO NOTES TO HAVE, MORE TEST DONE.

MAY 12, 2004 PAIN, NOTES I HAVE BEEN IN THE EMERGENCY ROOM MULTIPLE TIMES FOR PAIN AND OTHER. ITS NOTED I AM CONCERNED ABOUT PANCREATIC CANCER BECAUSE OF ALL THE PAINS AND NOTES MY UNCLE DIED FROM. HAD URINARY TROUBLES ALSO. NOW SHOWS ALL THE ABOVE AND HISTORY OF UTI. MY DOCTOR MAKES A NOTE THAT MY SYMPTOMS ARE EXAGGERATED BY THE ANXIETY. I WONDER WHY. I'AM HAVING TROUBLE AND DON'T KNOW WHATS GOING ON.

MAY 26, 2004 <u>HOSPITAL VISIT</u>—FLANK PAIN NOW FOR 6-7 MONTHS OFF AND ON—HAD A CT SCAN OF THE ABDOMEN AND PELVIS

JUNE 1, 2004 <u>HOSPITAL VISIT</u>—TEST DONE SAYS HEMATURIA ON <u>I.V.P. EXAM</u>

JUNE 4, 2004 NOTED WILL DISCONTINUE <u>STATIN DRUG # 1</u>. THE PATIENT IS AT EXTREMELY HIGH RISK FOR CEREBROVASCULAR AND CARDIOVASCULAR COMPLICATIONS ASSSOCIATED WITH THE HYPERLIPIDEMIA. I WILL GIVE HIM (STATIN DRUG 2). ITS NOTED I WENT TO THE HOSPITAL AND THEY SAY GET OFF OF THE DRUG BECAUSE I WAS HAVING MULTIPLE SIDE EFFECTS ASSOCIATED WITH IT. ALSO HAD CT WHEN SHOWED BORDERLINE ABNORMALITY. THIS IS WHEN I WAS SCHEDULED TO HAVE THE CYSTOSCOPY AS EARLIER PLANNED. OTHER BLOOD WORK WAS ALSO DONE. I WAS ON <u>ANTI IFLAMITORY DRUG</u> AGAIN AT THIS TIME, NOT KNOWING OF ITS SIDE AFFECTS ALSO. THERES NOTES OF CPK, MM, MB, DONE.

JULY 7, 2004 NOTES COMPLAINING OF FREQUENCY AND DYSURIA. I HAVE A HISTORY OF CHRONIC HEMATURIA. I HAVE ALSO BEEN SEEN MULTIPLE TIMES AT THE HOSPITAL EMERGENCY ROOM AND THERE, AND WAITING FOR ANOTHER APPOINTMENT WITH A UROLOGIST WHICH IS SCHEDULED FOR DECEMBER LATER THIS YEAR. NOTES URINALYSIS POSITIVE FOR HEMATURIA, BLOOD. NOW ALSO NOTES:
    CHRONIC HEMATURIA
    ANXIETY DISORDER
    PROSTATISM

THIS PAPER ALSO NOTES WILL ATTEMPT TO GET ME A SOONER APPOINTMENT WITH A UROLOGIST AND SEEMS TO THINK THIS IS BAD, BECAUSE OF THE WAY WROTE DOWN.

JULY 8, 2004 <u>HOSPITAL VISIT</u>—TEST DONE, EGD AND COLONOSCOPY, INDICATIONS: PEPTIC ULCER DISEASE, ON

THE COLON TEST NOTED SOME DIVERTICULOSIS ON LEFT COLON, DIDN'T KNOW I HAD A LEFT OR RIGHT COLON.

JULY 19, 2004 <u>HOSPITAL VISIT</u>—SHORT OF BREATH, HEAVYNESS IN THE CHEST, I JUST WANT TO SAY, DO YOU NOTICE THE NUMBER OF VISITS ALREADY TO HOSPITAL AND DOCTOR SINCE I STARTED ON THE NEW MEDICINES? THEY HAD GIVE ME SOMETHING FOR ANXEITY HERE

AUGUST 10, 2004 STILL HAVING MUSCLE PAINS AND SIDE ACHES, THIS IS WHAT I COME IN FOR CONTINUEING TROUBLE. THIS PAGE <u>NOW SHOWS A HISTORY OF ELEVATED CPK LEVEL ON STATINS</u>. I HAD DISCONTINUED <u>A STATIN DRUG</u> AT THIS TIME. AND NOTED REPEATED HIGH CPK LEVELS.

AUGUST 14, 2004 <u>HOSPITAL VISIT</u>—FLANK PAIN RADIATING TO BACK-X-RAYS—AND URINALYSIS HAS A NOTE BRONCIHTIS AND BLOOD IN URINE

SEPTEMBER 8, 2004 NOTES OF UROLOGY AS SCHEDULED, I AM ADVISED TO CONTINUE TO LOSING WEIGHT AND EXERCISE. I HAD TOLD HIM I WAS HAVING TROUBLE WITH THIS BECAUSE OF WALKING PAIN, AND NOT KNOWING AT THAT TIME THE MEDICINES WERE HELPING WITH THIS. ALSO NOTED WAS TO GIVE A NEW COLESTEROL MED, <u>XXX</u> IN THE NEAR FUTURE. I MUST HAVE TOLD HIM I WAS SURE THE PROBLEMS WERE THE CHOLESTEROL MEDS AT THIS TIME.

SEPTEMBER 17, 2004 <u>HOSPITAL VISIT</u>—BLOOD IN URINE

OCT. 21, 2004 <u>HOSPITAL VISIT</u>—BREATHING TROUBLE, LAB WORK DONE, EKG, OX @ 98%
X-RAY DONE, NOTED DYSPNEA, CHOUGH WHEEZE ON PAPER, THERE WAS SOMETHING NOTED ON THE PAPER I DON'T UNDERSTAND.

NOVEMBER 11, 2004 <u>HOSPITAL VISIT</u>—SHOULDER PAIN AGAIN

NOVEMBER 12, 2004 MUSCLE PAINS AGAIN, THIS TIME I STATE PAIN MEDICINE IS NOT WORKING. MORE BLOOD TEST TO SHOW HIGH CPK LEVELS.

DEC 3, 2004 **HOSPITAL VISIT**—VISIT FOR PAIN, ALMOST A YEAR TO DATE AT HOSPITAL AGAIN

DEC 21, 2004 **HOSPITAL VISIT**—UROLOGY CLINIC-CHECK FOR BLOOD AGAIN IN URINE

JANUARY 13, 2005 NOW COMPLAINS OF FAINTING SPELLS, FEELS LIKE I WANT TO PASS OUT. I CAN'T MAKE OUT ANY OTHER WRITING.

JANUARY 27, 2005 **HOSPITAL VISIT**—MUSCLESKELETAL PAIN-DIAGNOSIS (WHICH I STILL HAVE A LOT OF)

FEBUARY 10, 2005 TALKS ABOUT LAB WORK. I SEE NAN 500 NOTED TAKEN AT THIS TIME.(ANOTHER STATIN DRUG)

MARCH 22, 2005 **HOSPITAL VISIT**—NOT RELATED TO MEDICINES AND MAYBE THE ONLY ONE? I GOT GLASS IN EYE

APRIL 7, 2005 **HOSPITAL VISIT**—KIDNEY PAIN AND BLOOD AGAIN-NOTE I'AM STILL ON THE CHOLESTEROL MEDS. THERE WERE X-RAYS THAT NOTED THICKENING OF THE BLADDER WALL AND OTHER

APRIL 15, 2005 COME IN FOR MORE PAIN TROUBLE.

JUNE 1, 2005 FIRST TIME THE EYES RED IS TALKED ABOUT, MORE PAIN IN MANY PLACES AND BREATHING TROUBLE.

SEPTEMBER 29 2005 TALKS ABOUT THE WHOLE BODY WEAKNESS NOW, ACHING PAIN AND CHEST PAIN. STEADY FOR 3 MONTHS.

OCT 25, 2005 <u>HOSPITAL VISIT</u>—UROLOGY CLINIC-CHECKUPS FINDINGS—BLOOD IN URINE

NOVEMBER 14, 2005 <u>HOSPITAL VISIT</u>—AGAIN SOMETHING NOT RIGHT WITH A X-RAY AND BLOOD IN URINE

JANUARY 9, 2005 <u>NOTES I DON'T WANT ANY STATIN DRUGS LIST FEW WAS ON. NOTED ALSO STILL SEEING UROLOGIST</u>, AND TROUBLES THIS VISIT ARE—WEAKNESS, DIZZINESS FOR WEEKS, WEAKNESS IN LEGS ALSO FEELING LIKE I WILL PASS OUT, HEADACHES, LITE BURNING IN URINATION.

JANUARY 11, 2006 <u>HOSPITAL VISIT</u>—LAB WORK AND MORE TROUBLES, DIZZYNESS

MARCH 21, 2006 CONTINUED MUSCLE ACHES NOTED. ALSO NOTED WANTING TO PUT ME ON THE NEXT COLESTEROL MEDICINE, ANOTHER STATIN AGAIN.

APRIL 16, 2006 <u>HOSPITAL VISIT</u>—CAN'T HARDLY STAND UP SO DIZZY, VERTIGO POSITIONED AND GIVEN MEDS, BUT DON'T HELP AND NO DRIVING PUT DOWN, SO I LOST WORK FOR A WHILE OFF AND ON JUST FROM THIS.

<u>ONE MORE NOTE. THIS IS NOT ALL THE OTHER HOSPITAL VISITS</u>, JUST ONE OF THEM AND THE DOCTOR, THIS IS ALSO WHERE I DIDN'T GET THE REST OF MY RECORDS, THERES A LOT MORE!! THIS WAS JUST AFTER I CALLED ONE DRUG COMPANY AND THEY SAID THEY WOULD GIVE ME COMPANSATION BUT I LOST THE INFOMATION AND THEY NEVER CALLED BACK. REMEMBER I WAS ON MORE BUT THIS WAS THE FIRST DRUG COMPANY CALLED I HAD PASSED OUT OR LOST ALL MOTOR CONTROL LATER AND HAD BEEN ON MANY OF THE OTHER DRUGS BY THIS TIME.

JUNE 7, 2006 HAVING TROUBLE BREATHING COUGH AND STUFFY NOSE. MILD WHEEZE. PUT ON INHAILER

JULY 2006 HAVING MORE BLOOD IN URINE THAT YOU CAN SEE, ALSO PAINS IN KIDNEY AREA ON BACK. BACK TO THE UROLIGIST, AND MENTIONS CYSTOSOPY AGAIN. MORE PAIN!!!

AUGUST 10, 2006 MORE TROUBLES, PAIN IN LEFT SIDE OF BACK, ALSO HARD TO BREATHE.

LATER IN YEAR CAN MAKE OUT DATE: MORE TROUBLE ON TWO CHARTS, BOWELS ARE TALKED ABOUT HAVING TROUBLE, AND HURTING, CHRONIC KNEE PAIN, MORE MEDS AND BLOOD IN URINE.

MARCH 22, 2007 FIRST TIME OF HAVING A DAY OF FEELING GOOD, THIS IS MENTIONED ON A DOCTOR VISIT.

MAY 14, 2007 MORE HEADACHES, PUT ON NEW CHOLESTEROL MEDICINE, ALSO HAD A CT SCAN OF MY HEAD. DID'T SEE ANYTHING? ALSO SAYS I GOT OFF OF 1—DRUG THE HIGHER DOSE OF BLOOD PRESSURE MEDICINE. BLOOD PRESSURE HAD BEEN DROPPING DON'T NEED AS MUCH MEDICINE, MUST HAVE DONE SOMETHING RIGHT? OR WAS THE MEDICINE DOING SOMETHING TO BRING DOWN BLOOD PRESSURE IN A BAD WAY, DON'T KNOW, I HOPE SO & NOT MEDICINE DOING SOMETHING BAD TO BRING DOWN. PUT ON ANOTHER DRUG FOR BLOOD PRESSURE.

SEPTEMBER 29,2007 BAD SORE THROAT AND COUGHING. MORE MEDICINE.

JANUARY 8, 2008 TROUBLE SWALLOWING, DARK STOOLS, BAD HEARTBURN AGAIN. MORE TEST. EGD AT LCMC.

FEBUARY 25, 2008 MORE ANXIETY ATTACKS AND BAD, BURNING SENSATION TO CHEST FOR FEW DAYS. CHEST DISCOMFORT, TROUBLE BREATHING, HEAD FEEL LIKE ELECTRICITY IN SIDE-FLUSHING-CHEST DISCOMFORT—MORE LAB WORK, AND CAN NOT MAKE OUT ALL THE WRITING.

APRIL 14, 2008 MORE ANXIETY ATTACKS, PALPATIONS ITCHY THROAT, CONGESTION—<u>NOTES UNABLE TO TAKE STATINS AGAIN</u>, MUST HAVE GOT OFF ANOTHER ONE. CAN'T MAKE OUT ALL OF NOTES.

JULY 7, 2008 NOTES PAIN IN R—KNEE AND L—HIP, NOTES AT BOTTOM ABOUT THE WASP STING AND HAD ALLERGIC REACTION, PEN PROVIDED. <u>ALSO NOTES I CAN NOT TAKE STATINS AND NAMES ONE OF THE CHOLESTEROL MEDS</u>

AUGUST 20,2008 NOTES SWELLING TO RIGHT EYE, REDNESS IN EYE. NOTES ALLERGIC REACTION TO SOMETHING I HAVE TAKEN? HARD TO READ ALL OF THIS.

NOV. 20, 2008 CAN'T READ ALL BUT NOTES TO NASAL TROUBLE, AND POLYP'S. NOTE: I WAS NEVER TOLD ABOUT THE POLYPS, BUT WONDERED IF I HAD BECAUSE OF THE BREATHING TROUBLE OR BLOCKED NASAL PASSAGE ALL THE TIME, AND MEDICINE DON'T ALWAYS HELP.

MAY 9, 2009 BACK PAINS, LEG PAINS AGAIN, LEFT AND RIGHT. GIVES ME PAIN MEDICINE ONE OF THE ONES I HAD TROUBLE WITH LATER AND SENT TO HOSPITAL. ALSO SAYS I STILL HAVE GERD. AND <u>TAKEING ANTI ACID PILL</u>. CAN'T NAME THIS DRUG BUT FOR MY STOMACH, AND ONE OF FEW THAT HELPED ME ONE WAY BUT HURT ANOTHER.

AUGUST24, 2009 LAB—ROUTINE

DEC.3,2009 SHORT OF BREATH AGAIN, WEAKNESS, DIZZINESS.

MARCH 3, 2010 ROUTINE

SEPTEMBER 2010 THIS WAS THE WEAK SPELL I HAD AND WAS WEAK ON MY RIGHT LEG, I WENT DOWN WRONG AND PUT WEIGHT ON LEFT LEG AT SAME TIME WAS TWISTED, DIDN'T FEEL TO GOOD.

THIS DOES NOT INCLUDE ALL NOTES, BUT GIVES YOU AN IDEA OF MENTAL HORROR, PAIN, TROUBLE, COST, LOST OF MY HEATH & MY WORK, ALL BECAUSE OF CHOLESTEROL MEDICINES. PLEASE NOTE THAT AS I GOT OFF AND WAS OFF THE MEDS LONGER, THE TIMES BETWEEN VISITS ARE FURTHER APART. FACT!! STILL DON'T FEEL THE SAME BUT BETTER THAN I DID WHEN ON ALL THESE MEDICINES, ANOTHER FACT!

I DON'T REMEMBER SEEING WHEN I WAS GIVEN THIS DRUG XXX, I THINK THIS WAS ABOUT THE TIME OF XXX, I WAS GIVEN XXX AT DIFFERENT TIMES AND FOR DIFFERENT THINGS BEFORE I STOPPED TAKING IT. THIS ALSO INCLUDES OTHER MEDICINES WAS GIVEN OFF AND ON FOR WHAT REASON, I DON'T KNOW, THATS WHY THIS STORY OR A DOCUMENTARY OF WHAT HAPPENED SEEMS TO JUMP BACK AND FORTH.

JUST THINK OF ALL THE RADIATION AND CHEMICALS I HAVE BEEN EXPOSED TO. IS THIS MORE THAN I SHOULD HAVE BEEN EXPOSED TO? YES!!!! I MAY NEVER KNOW IF THAT CAUSES MORE TROUBLE IN THE FUTURE. BUT I CAN SAY AS OF JAN.31,2012 I STILL HAVE TROUBLES.

COST OF ALL THIS

I FIGURE I HAVE ABOUT 20-40,000.00 DOLLARS MORE OR LESS, IF I HAD TO PAY ALL OF THIS, THE STATE MAKES ME PAY SOME. <u>THIS IS NOT ALL THE TEST</u>, I HAD SOME TEST DONE I WAS TOLD WERE VERY EXPENSEIVE.

LETS DO THIS, I FIGURE I TALKED TO 5-600 PEOPLE OVER THE YEARS WHO TOLD ME THEY HAD TROUBLE WITH THIS MEDICINE, LETS SAY THERE RIGHT.

LETS PUT 20,000.00 DOLLARS
X   500 PEOPLE JUST IN MY 50 MILE RADIUS

10,000,000.00 DOLLARS THE STATE PUT OUT

X 50 STATES, YOU GOT A LOT OF MONEY. THIS IS WHY STATES NEED MONEY, FOR STUFF LIKE THIS AND ITS NOT MY FAULT, OR THERES. THIS IS JUST ABOUT COST GOING BY WHAT I WAS TOLD SOME TEST COST. ONE OF THE HOSPITALS I WENT TO SENT ME A BILL FOR THERE WORK, THIS WAS ONE VISIT, AROUND $3,200.00 THIS WAS WHEN I WORKED OFFSHORE AGAIN, AND STILL OWE THIS. THE AMBULANCE BILL WAS $1200.00, I ONLY OWE ABOUT $200.00 AT THE TIME OF THIS WRITING, AND FOR SOMETHING THAT WAS RELATED TO MEDICINE, DOCTOR SAID I WAS FULL OF CRAP, CONSTIPATED, MY MEDS WERE DOING THIS TO ME. MY WHOLE DIGESTIVE SYSTEM HASN'T BEEN THE SAME SINCE, FACT!!

I HAD TOLD A STATE REPRESENTIVE ABOUT THIS, I HEARD THEY WANTED TO CUT MONEY FROM THE HOSPITAL I WAS GOING TO AT THAT TIME. I TOLD HIM THIS AND IT MAKES

SENCE. WHEN A DRUG COMPANY IS FOUND TO HAVE A BAD DRUG ON THE MARKET AND THEY KNOW SOME OF THE PEOPLE WERE TREATED AT THIS HOSPITAL FOR THIS TROUBLE, THE DRUG COMPANYS NEED TO MAKE UP SOME OR ALL OF THE DIFFERENCE. THIS IS THE ONLY FAIR THING. EVEN IF ITS PART, WHERE DO I COME IN? I PAYED WITH MY HEALTH, AND MAY NEVER BE THE SAME. PLUS I STILL GET SOME BILLS FROM THE HOSPITAL AND I PAY THESE PLUS THE GAS TO DRIVE 80 MILE ROUND TRIP, AND YOU WONDER WHY PEOPLE CAN'T ALWAYS AFORD INSURANCE. ITS HARD SOMETIMES WHEN YOU'RE IN THE MIDDLE OF THE BIG HEALTH CARE MESS, BEING FORCED TO BUY INSURANCE WILL NOT HELP AT ALL, THIS IS WHAT I'AM TOLD THE NEW SYSTEM WILL BE SOON. AGAIN I'AM THE ONE PAYING WITH MY HEALTH, WHILE SOMEONES MAKING MILLIONS ON MY POOR HEALTH THAT I THINK THEY MAY HAVE CREATED. IF THIS ALONE WAS CORRECTED MORE TESTING OF MEDICINES THERE WOULD BE NO HEALTH CARE MESS, AT LEAST IN MY EYES, AND IF YOU HAD TROUBLE LIKE ME, I THINK YOU WOULD SAY THE SAME.

I WAS ALSO TOLD AT THE HOSPITAL, EVERY TIME I WOULD GO AND THEY SAY WE CAN'T FIND ANYTHING BUT I'AM HURTING LIKE I DON'T KNOW WHAT, OR HAVING SOME KIND OF TROUBLE, WE DO NOT DO TEST FOR CANCER UNLESS AT LEAST 5 DOCTORS THINK ITS SO. I KNOW SOME ONE WHO WENT THOUGHT THIS, OVER AND OVER HAD TROUBLE, HE WAS SENT HOME. HE WENT TO ANOTHER HOSPITAL OUT OF TOWN, STATE RUN ALSO HE WAS IN STAGE 4 CANCER. HE IS STILL HAVING THINGS DONE AND I DON'T KNOW IF LEVELED OUT, FROM WHAT I UNDER STAND, YES HES' OK SO FAR.

JUST THINK OF THE COST IF I HAD TO GET OR NEED LATER A TRANSPLANT, BECAUSE SOMETHING WHEN OUT. THAT'S IF I'AM LUCKY AND DON'T DIE FIRST BEFORE GETING A ORGAN IF I EVEN CAN GET ONE. I THINK THIS ALL THE TIME BECAUSE I JUST DON'T KNOW WHAT THESE MEDS DONE TO ME. I JUST KNOW I STILL HURT, SOMETIMES ALL OVER, AND I'AM STILL WEAK.

I WENT TO DO YARD WORK TODAY Sunday, September 26, 2010, WAS ONLY WORKING ABOUT 10-15 MINUTES AND HAD TO STOP. I WAS ALREADY GETING WEAK AND DIZZY. JUST CAN'T TAKE THE HEAT.

AFTER ALL THIS, IF THIS DIDN'T CAUSE A LOT OF TROUBLE THEN YOU HAVE THE HOSPITALS TURNING YOU IN TO COLLECTION SERVICE AND THE ONLY BUSSNESS THAT DIDN'T, THE WHOLE TIME I WAS PAYING WAITED UNTIL I WAS ALMOST FINISHED PAYING AND TURNED ME IN. HOW LOW CAN YOU GET. THE BILL WAS JUST OVER $1200.00 AND I HAD PAID ALL BUT 149.00 AND FEW CENTS I WAS JUST TURNED IN, JUST BEFORE THIS BOOK WENT TO PRESS. THE AMBULANCE SERVICE I HAD TO CALL WHEN I WAS ON THE BOAT OR THE DAY I GOT OFF BECAUSE OF SICKNESS. I HAD TALKED TO THEM AND THEY AGREEDED TO HELP ME AND WORK THIS OUT AND LET ME PAY AS MUCH AS I CAN. THE GREED IN THERE BUSSNESS ACTIONS TOOK OVER AFTER ME ALMOST PAYING OUT THE FULL BALANCE. THIS IS NOT THE FIRST OR ONLY ONE. ONE LOCAL HOSPITAL DIDN'T EVEN SEND A BILL OR LET ME TRY TO PAY. IT BYPASSED ME AND WENT DIRECT TO THE COLLECTION AGENCY. THIS IS AGAIN ALL THE HORRORS I HAVE TO GO THROUGH. IN LOUISIANNA THERE IS A LAW THAT SAYS A VERBAL AGREEMENT IS THE SAME AS A WROTE OUT AGREEMENT. I HAD BOTH ON PAPER AND VERBAL BUT WAS STILL TURNED IN. IF MORE COMPANYS WOULD WORK WITH THE PEOPLE THAT ARE TRUELY TRYING TO PAY BILLS, THIS COUNTRY WOULD BE MORE AT PEACE. AND NO COMPANY SHOULD BE ABLE TO SELL THERE DEBT TO ANOTHER TO TAKE MORE MONEY FROM YOU. THIS KEEPS PUTTING AMERICANS MORE IN THE HOLE. I DON'T KNOW IF THEY DO, OR DON'T, BUT I'LL ALMOST BET THEY NOT ONLY GET A TAX BREAK, BUT WRITE THE DEBT OFF. IF THIS IS TRUE, THEN IT SHOULD NOT BE A DOUBLE BILL.

I OWED A ELECTRONIC STORE $200.00 FOR A VCR YEARS BACK, LOST MY JOB, TRYED TO PAY EVERY BODY AND BEGED THEM TO WORK WITH ME I WOULD PAY THEM BACK. I ALMOST

FILED FOR BANKRUPTCY, BUT DIDN'T AT LAST MINUTE. TO PUT IT SHORT BUY THE TIME I STARTED WORKING AGAIN AND GOT THE BANK TO PAY ALL THE BILLS OFF AND HAVE ONE NOTE. I OWED ABOUT $1,200.00 TO A MAJOR STORE FOR A $200.00 VHS VCR. THEY ADDED LATE FEES, INTREST FEES AND WHAT EVER THEY COULD FEES, IT SEEMS LIKE ANYWAY. NOW THE CHOLESTEROL MEDICINES JUST BRING THE SAME THING BACK. WILL I EVER GET A BREAK? I KNOW I AM NOT PERFECT BUT I ALWAYS DID TRY TO NOT ONLY PAY ON TIME, BUT PAY OFF EARY WHEN I COULD, AND I AM NOT THE ONLY ONE WITH THESE TROUBLES, AND I FEEL SO SORRY FOR THE ONES WHO MAY HAVE IT WORST THAN ME. ALL I CAN SAY IS, WRITE ABOUT IT, TELL EVERY ONE WHAT HAPPENED. WHERE ARE THE LAWS TO PROTECT THE ONES WHO AT LEAST TRY TO PAY, I KNOW I HELPED THE BAIL OUT. MAYBE IF I OWED MORE THEY WOULD HAVE BAILED ME OUT, YEA, RIGHT.

THERE NEEDS TO BE A BALANCE, I SAY NO MORE THAN 15-20% OF WHAT YOU MAKE IN SAVINGS AND PAY FOR A LOAN. I'LL STOP HERE I DON'T WANT TO UPSET ANYONE.

IF I CAN FIND THIS MUCH HASSEL IN MY RING OF LIFE, WHAT ABOUT THE USA, AND OTHER AREAS. LETS' GET AWAY FOR A LITTLE BIT. I SEE THINGS ALL OVER THE WORLD AND I THINK WHY DONT THEY DO THIS OR THAT. ONE DAY MAYBE I CAN. I IF I LIVE LONG ENOUGH I WANT EVERY STATE SENATOR TO VOTE TO MAKE THIS HAPPEN, A SMALL PERCENT OF THE DRUG COMPANYS PROFITS GO TO PAY EACH STATE HOSPITALS BILLS WHEN THEY HAVE A DRUG TAKEN OFF THE MARKET AND IT IS KNOWN TO HAVE TREATED A PERSON LIKE ME FOR TROUBLES THAT DRUG HAS CAUSED. THIS IS FAIR TO THE PEOPLE OF EACH STATE WHO PAY THOSE TAXES AND THE PERSON WHO HAS NO INSURANCE AND IS SICK FROM DRUGS NOT THE BODY GIVING UP FROM NORMAL AGE PROBLEMS, THESE DRUGS AND OTHERS ADVANCE AGE RELATED TROUBLE OR CAUSE TROUBLE THAT THEY MAY NOT HAVE GOT FROM AGING.

FINANCAL STRESS

I APPLIED FOR A LOAN 2 DAYS AGO & TODAY NOV.18,2010 I FOUND OUT I HAD TO MANY COLLECTIONS ON MY NAME, <u>THESE WERE MEDICAL COLLECTIONS I WAS TOLD</u>. THE HOSPITAL SENT MY BILL DIRECT TO COLLECTION WITHOUT EVEN LETING ME TRY TO PAY SOME. THE HOSPITAL IN ANOTHER TOWN, LET ME PAY SOME BEFORE TURNING ME IN. THIS WAS THE TIME I WAS OFFSHORE AND HAD TO COME IN OFF NEW JOB, I WAS TAKING A DRUG THAT WAS JUST ON TV TO BE REMOVED FROM THE MARKET THAT MADE MY STOMACH TROUBLES WORSE. I PAY MY BILLS OK AND ON TIME WHEN I DON'T FORGET, BUT YOU HAVE THOSE TIMES WHEN NOT SURE TO PAY THIS OR THAT BILL AND HOLD ON TO MONEY A LITTLE LONGER TO MAKE SURE YOU WILL HAVE MONEY FOR THE MAIN BILLS, LIGHTS, WATER, GAS FOR WORK, CAR INSURANCE. THIS IS WHAT I CALL THE MAIN BILLS, PHONE AND CABLE LAST AND OTHERS, OFF COURSE YOU TRY TO PAY EVERYTHING AND DO, BUT THERE WHERE TIMES WHEN THE MEDICINES TOOK MY WORK DAYS AND MONEY FOR GAS AWAY. THIS ALONG WITH TAKING MEDICINES I NEEDED TO CONTROL THE TROUBLE I WAS HAVING NOT KNOWING AT THE TIME IF I WOULD HAVE STOPPED THE MEDICINES, THE MONEY WOULD STAY LONGER IN THE BANK. YOU REMEMBER THE AMULANCE SERVICE. THEY LET ME PAY ALL BUT 250-150 BEFORE TURNING ME IN FOR COLLECTIONS. THE LOAN I WAS TRYING TO GET WAS TO PAY SOME HIGH INTREST LOANS SO I COULD PAY MORE ON THERES AND GET A LOWER RATE DOING. THE MAIN POINT OF ALL, <u>IF I HAD NOT TAKEN ANY OF THESE MEDICINES I WOULD NOT BE IN POOR HEALTH WRITING THIS BOOK. AND WOULD STILL HAVE ALL THAT MONEY I GOT FROM MY DADS DEATH, AND THE LAND I WAS LEFT AND BOUGHT FROM MY STEPMOTHER.</u>

I WOULD BE WORKING A HIGHER PAYING JOB, I DO LIKE MY JOB NOW BUT I COULD BE MAKING MORE IF I DIDN'T HAVE SO MANY HEALTH TROUBLES. I ALSO WOULD STILL BE A NO SICK PERSON I'AM SURE OF THAT.

ANOTHER DAY
ANOTHER PAIN! & PILL

FRIDAY MORNING ABOUT 10AM AUGUST 6,2010, HAVING A WEAK SPELL WAS GOING TO EAT BREAKFAST & TAKE THE DOG FOR A RIDE, WHILE COMING DOWN THE STAIRS MY WEAK SPELL STARTED, MY RIGHT KNEE STARTED HURTING PLUS WAS KINDA WEAK, STILL HAVING WEAK SPELLS FROM ALL THE MEDS I WAS ON EVEN NOW.

I WENT TO STEP ON THE GROUND THE LAST STEP BEFORE GOING TO THE CAR AND HAD A SUDDEN WEAKNESS & RIGHT KNEE GAVE WAY, MY LEFT COME DOWN FAST TO TAKE THE WEIGHT AND TWISTED WHEN I STEPPED ON A BOARD ON THE GROUND THAT MOVED A LITTLE I THINK. I WAS TRYING TO HOLD MY SELF FROM TWISTING BUT COULDN'T, HAD THE DOG IN MY HAND. I WAS IN BAD PAIN, COULD NOT PUT PRESSURE ON MY FOOT. I HAD TO CRAWL INTO MY HOUSE IT WASN'T UNTILL LATE THAT NIGHT I WAS ABLE TO WALK EASY ON IT. WENT TO THE DOCTOR SATURDAY MORNING DOCTOR GIVE ME A PAIN SHOT AND SOME MEDICINE TO HELP WITH THE PAIN AND INFLAMATION. SOMETHING NOT RELATED BUT TROUBLE, I HAD SOME AFTER LEAVING THE DOCTOR I TOOK THE OLD WAY HOME, MY TRUCK STARTED CUTTING OUT AND STOPPED, PULLED OFF ROAD, WOULD NOT START, I CALLED A WRECKER THINKING SOMETHING BAD, TURNS OUT GAS GAGE OFF, OUT OF GAS. BUT ITS KINDA HOT AND NOW THE PAIN MEDICINE IS STARTING TO KICK IN. IF A POLICE WOULD HAVE COME HE WOULD HAVE THOUGHT I WAS DRUNK I COULD HARDLY WALK BY THE TIME THE WRECKER COME. I MADE IT HOME AND WAITED TILL LATER MONDAY TO TAKE THE MEDICINE, AS YOU READ IN THE BOOK, I'AM TO PILL SHY ON

ALMOST ANY PILL NOW. MONDAY TOOK THE PAIN MEDICINE ABOUT 2:30-3AM THAT MORNING DIDN'T HELP WITH THE PAIN INSTEAD HAD A REACTION TO THE MEDICINE, WOKE UP NOT FEELING RIGHT, BY NOON WAS HAVING TROUBLE BREATHING, WENT TO DRUG STORE TO GET INFORMATION ON THE PAIN MEDICINE I WAS ON, LOOKED AS IF I WAS HAVING A ALERGIC REACTION TO THE PAIN MEDICINE. AROUND 2:30 GOT MY SISTER TO BRING ME TO THE HOSPITAL IN HOUMA, 40 MILES AWAY. BY THIS TIME WAS GASPING FOR AIR TOLD HER TO CALL MY BROTHER, I DIDN'T THINK I WAS GOING HOME, I JUST NEW I WAS DIEING.

THE DOCTOR SAW ME AROUND 4:30 PM AND GIVE ME SOME BENIDRIL TO HELP, BY 6:00 PM I WAS DOING OK, AND RESTING AND BREATHING OK. THIS WAS A 12 HR MEDICINE AND WAS JUST OVER 12 HOURS BEFORE IT WAS STARTING TO WEAR OFF. THE DOCTOR GIVE ME SOME OTHER PAIN MEDICATION. A COMMON BRAND IS WHAT I TOOK, THIS IS THE SAME DRUG TAKEN FEW YEARS BEFORE AND HAD NO TROUBLE WITH.

DID I MENION I LOST 2 DAYS OF WORK ALSO. I WORK WHERE I MUST GO UP & DOWN STAIRS AND IS PAINFUL STILL TODAY OVER WEEK LATER, AUG 14, 2010. MY DOCTOR HASN'T TOLD ME HOW BAD MY KNEE IS YET, SAID TO CALL IN A WEEK.

YOU MAY HAVE READ HOW I HAD A ALERGIC REACTION TO A BEE STING. I WAS ALSO HAVING TROUBLE SWALLOWING, WITH THE ABOVE TROUBLES AND WITH THE BEE STING. I BELIEVE IT WAS THE SATIN DRUG I WAS ON WHEN THIS STARTED. ONE OF THE CHOLESTEROL MEDICINES CAUSES ALERGYS. I GOT TROUBLES NOW, I NEVER HAD TO WORRY ABOUT BEFORE, I HAVE TO NOW.

THIS IS A CONTINUING SAGA OF WHAT I'AM STILL HAVING TO LIVE WITH BECAUSE OF PERMANENT INJURY TO ME AND MY BODY FROM ALL THE MEDICINES I TOOK. AND IT ALL STARTED WITH TAKING CHOLESTEROL MEDICINES, AND THE

OTHER MEDS, TO COUNTER REACT THOSE SIDE AFFECTS, PLUS THE SIDE AFFECTS OF THOSE MEDS.

EVERY THING I HAVE WROTE ABOUT HAPPENED TO ME AND OTHERS I TALKED TO I SAY WHAT THEY TOLD ME, I HEAR TROUBLE ALL THE TIME. TODAY SOMEONE ASKED ME IF I WAS DOING BETTER, TOLD THEM I WAS STILL WEAK AND WAS HAVING JOINT PAINS, HE TOLD ME HE HAD STARTED HAVING SOME OF THE SAME TROUBLES, HE WAS ON CHOLESTEROL MEDS FOR ABOUT 5 YEARS BUT DID NOT TAKE A HIGH DOSE LIKE I DID. YOU CAN FIND MORE STORYS, AND ALL THIS ON THE INTERNET OTHER PEOPLE WITH THE SAME OR SIMULAR TROUBLE, I'VE DONE A LOT OF SEARCHING ON THE NET AND RESEARCH ON MY OWN PROBLEMS, AND THE COMPANYS ARE SHOWING TROUBLES I WAS NEVER TOLD ABOUT, WHEN I WAS FIRST HAVING TROUBLE, MY DOCTOR LOOKED AT ME LIKE I WAS NUTS, WHEN I WOULD TELL HIM OF WEARD THINGS HAPPENING TO ME, WELL OTHER PEOPLE TOLD ME THE SAME, THERE DOCTOR DID'NT BELIEVE THEM. WELL THIS BOOK IS TO LET IT ALL OUT, YOUR NOT NUTS, WHATS YOUR TROUBLE? TELL SOMEONE IF YOU THINK YOUR MEDICINE IS GIVING YOU TROUBLE, YOU KNOW YOUR BODY MORE THAN YOUR DOCTOR, HE DOES'NT KNOW WHAT YOU FEEL, ONLY YOU CAN TELL HIM OR HER HOW YOU FEEL. IF YOU GET MAD ITS OK, MAYBE HE WILL START BELIEVING YOU IF YOU TELL HIM TO TAKE THE DRUGS HIMSELF, LIKE THE DOCTORS I TALKED TO.

THE END PART

I HAD SEEN ON TV NOT LONG AGO, A DRUG THAT SEEMS TO BE FOR ANXIETY AND SAYS MAY RAISE YOUR CHOLESTEROL LEVELS. I'AM NOT A DOCTOR, BUT I DO HAVE MORE COMMON SENCE THAN SOME PEOPLE I WILL NOT SAY WHO. IF I'AM GIVEN THE INFORMATION I GOT ON TV, AND THE ANXIETY DRUGS DO RAISE THE LEVELS UP MORE, AND THE DOCTORS SAYS NOW WE HAVE TO GO UP ON YOUR DOSE OR EVEN START. THIS DOES NOT MAKE ANY SENCE TO TAKE AT ALL, WHEN THERES THE SIDE AFFECT THAT WILL PUT YOU ON THE OTHER MEDICATIONS. CHANGE YOUR DIET, NOW. FIND OUT WHAT FOODS YOU EAT THAT ARE HIGH IN CHOLESTEROL, STOP EATING OR AT LEAST DO WHAT I DO, DON'T EAT SOME OF THOSE FOODS AS OFTEN, YOU KNOW THAT YOU WILL STILL EAT ANYWAY . . . YOUR HUMAN. THE INFORMATION IN MY BOOK IS BASED ON WHAT HAPPENED TO ME AND FEW OTHERS THAT TOLD ME THERE HORROR STORYS, I KNOW I TALKED TO OVER 600 PEOPLE FROM 45-90 ONLY ONE LADY TOLD ME SHE TOOK CHOLESTEROL MEDICINE AND DID NOT HAVE ANY TROUBLE, BUT LATER SHE DID SAY SHE DID NOT TAKE HER MEDICINE EVERY DAY AND WHEN SHE LEFT I SAW HER LIMPING, I ASKED' WHAT HAPPENED HOW SHE GOT HURT, SHE SAID SHE JUST STARTED HAVING JOINT PAINS, WELL IF YOUR THINKING WHAT I DID, YOU KNOW. I'AM NOT SAYING TO NOT TAKE ANYTHING YOUR DOCTOR GIVES YOU. JUST PLEASE USE YOUR COMMON SENCE. YOU AND ONLY YOU CAN TELL IF YOUR GETING BETTER OR WORSE, IF YOU NOTICE ANY CHANGES IN PAIN, MORE OR LESS. MAKE NOTES, IF YOUR LIKE ME WHEN YOU SEE THE DOCTOR, YOU TEND TO FORGET SOME OF THE THINGS THAT HAPPENED. MAKE YOUR OWN NOTES AND MAKE SURE HE NOTES THESE THINGS, THE REASON, I TALKED TO ONE OF THE LAWYERS ON TV, IF

YOUR DOCTOR DOES NOT NOTE THINGS, ITS LIKE IT DIDN'T HAPPEN IF HE DIES AND YOU HAVE TO GET A NEW DOCTOR, I WAS TOLD MY OLD RECORDS FROM MY CHILDHOOD MAY OR MAY NOT EXIST ANYMORE. THERE SHOULD BE A LAW WHERE IF A DOCTOR DIES ALL YOUR MEDICAL RECORDS GO TO YOU, FOR YOUR NEW DOCTOR. BECAUSE I DIDN'T SEE A DOCTOR BUT ONCE TO TWICE A YEAR, I NEVER THOUGHT OF THIS, BUT I DO NOW.

IF IT SEEMS LIKE I JUMPED BACK AND FORTH WITH WHAT HAPPENED, THATS BECAUSE OF SOMETIMES ONE DRUG MAY HAVE NOT DONE AS BAD AS THE ONE BEFORE OR AFTER. ALSO I WAS GIVEN DIFFERENT DRUGS TO TRY FOR MORE OR LESS MONEY. BUT EVEN THE CHEAPER ONES DIDN'T ALWAYS WORK. SOME OVER THE COUNTER ACID REDUCER DRUGS DID WORK VERY WELL AND FAST. I LIKED THE OVER COUNTER CHEWABLE ANTI ACID DRUG. BUT FOUND OUT ON MY OWN, I COULD NOT TAKE WHEN ON OTHER ACID REDUCER DRUGS, MY EYES WOULD GET BLOOD RED, IT DID NOT HURT ME ANYWAY THAT I KNOW OF BUT LOOKED HORRIBLE AND DO NOT KNOW IF THIS LIKE ALL THE OTHER THINGS THAT HAPPEND DAMAGED MY BODY FOR LIFE, OR SHORTED MY LIFE.

THE ONLY PILLS I TAKE NOW ARE MY BLOOD PRESSURE AT 5 MG, IF I HAVE ANY STOMACH FLARE UPS THE ACID REDUCER PILL IS HIGH ON MY LIST OR A QUICK CHEWABLE TABLET, AND I DON'T LEAVE HOME WITHOUT MY ANXIETY MEDS. JUST INCASE. I REALY WANT TO NOTE THAT ANY MONEY MADE FROM THIS IS TO NOT ONLY HELP ME WITH THE MEDICIAL BILLS AND OTHER TEST I STILL NEED, BUT WILL USE TO HELP OTHERS, I SEE PEOPLE ALL THE TIME <u>THAT NEED THERE MEDICINES.</u> ONE OF MY OWN RELATIVES DIED ON CHRISTMAS EVE ON HIS WAY TO SEE HIS SISTER, WE WERE TOLD HE HAD TRIED TO CUT BACK ON HIS MEDICINES, HE HAD A HEART ATTACK ON THE ROAD AND RUN OFF, WITNESSES SAY HE JUST HUMPED OVER THE STEERING WHEEL BEFORE HE RAN OFF THE ROAD NEAR BATON ROUGE, LA. I HAVE TO SAY,

SOME MEDICINES WE DO NEED. ANY THING FOR CANCER AND LIFE SAVING DRUGS WE NEED, YES I WOULD TRY IF I DID NEED A LIFE SAVING DRUG, BUT ONE JUST TO BETTER LIFE, HOPE THEY DO GOOD RESEARCH ON. IF YOU NEED MEDICINES AND YOU CAN'T DO ANYTHING WITH OUT FINE, BUT WHEN ITS A SIMPLE LIFE CHANGE IN HABITS, CHANGE YOUR HABITS FIRST. REMEMBER DRUGS ARE THERE TO HELP, BUT YOU CAN HELP TO IN SOME CASES. LOOK UP THE FACTS, TALK TO YOUR DOCTOR, IF HE'S NOT SURE LOOK UP ON THE NET. THERES A LOT OF GOOD INFORMATION TO KEEP YOU INFORMED. SEARCH ENGINES ARE A WONDERFUL THING ON THE NET.

DON'T BE DISCOURGED OF DRUGS, JUST BE VERY AWARE OF THE GOOD, AND THE BAD THEY CAN DO.

YOU CAN CALL THE FDA FOR INFORMATION, AND THAT'S ALL YOU'LL DO IS CALL. THEY NEVER CALLED ME BACK. ALL I WANTED WAS INFORMATION AT THE TIME. I ALSO WANT THIS BOOK TO BE A QUESTION OF WHY THIS HAPPENS TO OFTEN. I'AM ALL FOR NEW DRUGS TO HELP AND RESEARCH BUT SOME OF MY OWN RESEARCH I SAW SOMEWHERE WHERE ONE OF THE DRUGS I TOOK, WAS ONLY TESTED 4 MONTHS, THIS IS WHAT IT SHOWED. MY TROUBLES WERE JUST WARMING UP AT 4 MONTHS, I HOPE I MISSED SOMETHING BUT THIS IS WHAT IT SHOWED, 4 MONTHS. THERE NEEDS TO BE RESHEARCH FOR AT LEAST 5 YEARS MINIMUM. **ALL DRUGS NEED TO BE FOLLOWED ONCE RELEASED**, AND ANY SIDE AFFECT'S AND ALL SHOULD BE KNOWN TO THE PUBLIC, NOT JUST THOSE FEW. ONE COMPANYS PAPER I FOUND WITH THE MEDICINE HAD ALMOST ALL THE TROUBLES I HAD ON THERE BLUE SIDE AFFECT SHEET. THE DRUG STORE DID NOT HAVE ALL THESE THINGS ON THERE SHEET. I SHOULD ALSO NOTE THE SHEET OF SIDE AFFECTS WAS NOT PUT IN ALL THE BOXES I HAD, SO IF YOU HAPPEN TO GET SOME OF THESE DRUGS, THERES A CHANCE YOU MAY NOT GET THE PAPER I HAD. NOT ALL THE WRITING IS IN A WAY I CAN UNDER STAND, BUT THERE WAS ENOUGHT TO GET ME GOING IN THE RIGHT DIRECTION OF UNDERSTANDING WHAT HAPPENED TO ME, AND WHAT

TO LOOK FORWARD TO. I DON'T EVEN THINK I SAID I HAD
GAINED WEIGHT. I WAS A LITTLE OVER BUT WAS HAVING A
TIME TRING TO LOSE WEIGHT. MANY DRUGS I TOOK MAKE
YOU GAIN OR HOLD YOUR WEIGHT.

HAVING THE JOINT PAINS AND TRING TO WALK TO
LOSE WEIGHT DID NOT HELP AT ALL. THE MORE I WALKED
THE MORE I SUFFERED. THEN THE I CAN'T TAKE THE HEAT
ANYMORE WOULD KICK IN. IT SEEMS LIKE I'AM FIGHTING A
LOSING BATTLE. MY HEALTH LONG AND SHORT TERM I DON'T
KNOW WHAT WILL HAPPEN, AS I SAID BEFORE IN MY BOOK,
EVERY DAY REALY IS A NEW ADVENTURE.

LOST DREAMS

I WANT TO MENTION, SOMETHING NOT RELATED TO DRUGS,
BUT WE REALY NEED A GOVERMENT OVER HALL. CUT LARGE
SALARYS, I TRYED TO APPLY FOR A RADIO STATION FEW
YEARS AGO. THE FCC TURNED ME DOWN BECAUSE OF THE BIG
STATIONS COMPLAINING OF LOW POWER FM STATIONS. I
LIKE TO HELP PEOPLE I FELT I COULD DO A LOT WITH A RADIO
STATION. I LIKE THE MUSIC WE PLAYED BUT THE STATION I
WORKED FOR WAS SOLDED AND MOVED THE STUDIO OUT OF
TOWN, I DIDN'T WANT TO DRIVE 35-40 MILES AND AT THE
PRICE OF GAS, NO WAY. SO I DONE OTHER THINGS. ANY WAY
I WAS TURNED DOWN AT THE END BY FCC BECAUSE I MAILED
A LETTER OVERNIGHT AND THE POSTAL SERVICE SENT IT ON
A MONDAY AND NOT FRIDAY. I COLLECTED ALL THE RECORDS
FOR GOSPEL, OLDIES MUSIC ON CD, RECORDS. I HAD OLD
EQUIPMENT EVERYTHING BUT THE LICENSE AND A $1500.00
TRANSMITER. I CALLED THEY NEVER CALLED BACK OR SAID
ANYTHING. I CALLED THE POSTAL SERVICE, THEY SAID IT
SHOULD HAVE BEEN THERE EVEN IF THE ZIP WAS WRONG,
WHICH BY THE WAY THE POSTAL WORKER CHANGED AND
TOLD ME I HAD IT WRONG, I DIDN'T!!! FEDERAL BUILDINGS
HAVE THERE OWN ZIP CODE, THIS IS WHAT I WAS TOLD.

THE POINT IS YOU CAN LOSE DREAMS FROM DRUGS AND THE
PEOPLE THERE TO HELP SERVE YOU. STAND UP AND VOTE TO

MAKE CHANGES, USE COMMON KNOWLEGE, AND HOPE YOUR VOTING FOR THE RIGHT PERSON, OR IN THIS CASE, USEING SAFE DRUGS. ONLY YOU CAN HELP CHANGE THE WORLD TO MAKE BETTER. AND <u>PLEASE RECYCLE</u>.

HERE'S SOMETHING TO TRY FOR ONE WEEK OR A MONTH. I DONE THE MONTH THING. COLLECT ALL YOUR PLASTIC AND PUT IN A BIG GARBAGE BAG. YOU WILL BE SO SURPRISED HOW MUCH YOU COLLECT IN ONE MONTH OR EVEN A WEEK. WE DON'T NEED THIS IN THE WATERS OR LAND FILL. PLEASE JUST TRY ONE TIME.

THANKS, KENNETH

UPDATE: I CALLED FDA AGAIN AND THEY SENT ME A FORM TO FILL OUT, I DID TELL THEM TO READ THE BOOK BECAUSE THE SPACE THEY GIVE FOR TROUBLE IS WAY TO SMALL TO PUT ALL I WENT THROUGH. I SENT THIS IN A FEW DAYS AGO, TODAY IS JAN. 31, 2012

THE DIFFERENT DATES YOU MAY SEE IS FROM EACH TIME SOMETHING IS TYPED I PUT THE DATE AS OF THAT TIME, BUT EVERYTHING YOU READ HAPPENED TO ME AND I DO STILL HAVE HEALTH PROBLEMS THAT COME AND GO BUT NOT FOR LONG SPOTS OF TIME. I MAY FEEL GOOD LIKE SUNDAY, AND TODAY MADE A DOCTORS APOINTMENT FOR TOMORROW, BECAUSE OF MY STOMACH AND WEAKNESS, AND AGAIN HAD TO TAKE OFF WORK, LOSING MONEY ALL THE TIME, THEN YOU HAVE THE GAS AND COST OF THE DOCTOR AND MAYBE MORE TEST.

WHATS NEXT?

THE LETTER

JUST GOT A LETTER FROM ONE DRUG COMPANY AND THEY DONT WANT TO ASUME THEIR DAMAGE TO ME AND OTHER TROUBLES THEY GAVE ME. THEY DID SAY THERES CAUSES KIDNEY DAMAGE/TROUBLE BUT DID NOT SEE IT IN MY RECORDS, YOU READ THE RECORDS AND IN MY OWN WORDS AND THE DOCTORS TEST IN THERE OWN WORDS, HOW CRAZY IS THIS TRUE NIGHTMARE?

I DIDNT HAVE INTERNET FEW YEARS AGO TO LOOK UP MY TROUBLES TO VERIFY MOST OF MY TROUBLES WERE RELATED TO THE MEDS, BUT I DO NOW AND I AM FINDING THINGS OUT EVERY DAY, IF U TAKE MEDS, TRY TO LOOK UP YOUR MEDS, THIS MAY HELP YOU IN THE LONG RUN, SOME MEDS YOU HAVE TO TAKE EVERY DAY, BUT THERE IS A DIFFERENCE IN SOME MEDS THAT DO THE SAME THING. I JUST GOT A NEW PILL FOR BLOOD PRESSURE, SAME NAME DIFFERENT DRUG COMPANY AND ENDED UP IN PAIN AGIN FROM DRUGS, HAD TO GO BACK TO THE ORIGINAL MAKER, OF THE MEDICINE I WAS TAKING. ITS SMALL THINGS LIKE THIS THAT WILL DRIVE YOU CRAZY, YOU THINK YOU HAVE A NEW TROUBLE BUT IS DRUG RELATED. I DID CALL THE DRUG COMPANY AND THEY WANT THE MEDS BACK FOR TESTING TO SEE WHY I ENDED UP IN KINDNEY PAIN AND JOINT PAIN IN RIGHT HAND ONLY TWO FINGERS, WEARD BUT THIS HAPPENED JULY 2011, AFTER GETTING OFF MEDS AND BACK TO ORIGINAL PILL MOST OF MY PAIN WENT AWAY, AS I SAID IN THE BOOK, ANOTHER DAY ANOTHER PILL OR PAIN. I JUST HAD SOME CAT SCANS DONE AND NEEDING MORE, DON'T KNOW WHATS NEXT, CANCER DON'T KNOW, JUST KNOW TO MUCH TROUBLES THATS ALL RELATED TO PAST MEDS. AND ITS HARDER AND HARDER TO STAY AFLOAT. IF I COULD FIND THE RIGHT DOCTOR TO DO

THE RIGHT TEST, MAYBE SOMETHING GOOD COULD COME ABOUT. THIS I PRAY FOR.

I'VE SAID I HAVE AN ULCER, WHEN ON THE STATIN DRUGS HAD STOMACH TROUBLE TOLD ULCER, I DID HAVE A TEST AND DO HAVE AN ULCER, A VERY BAD ONE, THE DOCTOR DIDN'T SHOW ME THE PICTURE OF MINE BUT SHOWED ME A PICTURE AND SAID MINE WAS WORSE. THE PICTURE I SAW WAS A VERY BAD ULCER, MY LAST STOMACH TROUBLE THAT SEEM NOT TO GO AWAY THIS TIME STARTED JUNE 23,2011 AND I STILL BURN TODAY, MARCH 28, 2012 THAT'S ABOUT 8 MONTHS OF PAIN THAT DOESN'T SEEM TO WANT TO LEAVE. I'AM ON ANOTHER MEDICINE TO COAT STOMACH TO HELP HEAL WHAT THE OTHER MEDS MESSED UP. IF I DON'T HEAL UP YOU KNOW WHATS NEXT, DEATH FROM CANCER. JUST WHAT I'VE BEEN SAYING, IF IT DON'T HEAL AND STAYS RAW TO LONG IT CAN TURN TO CANCER, AND ALL OF THIS GOES BACK TO TAKING CHOLESTEROL MEDS OR STATIN DRUGS. A CONTINUEING NIGHTMARE OF PAIN, AND WORRY AND LOSING MY HEALTH BECAUSE I TOOK MEDS TO HELP ME LIVE LONGER? I DON'T THINK SO. I'AM ALSO HAVING TROUBLE GETTING LEGAL HELP, IF YOU ARE NOT DEAD YET NO ONE SEEMS TO WANT TO HELP.

KENNETH BOYNE

HERES A QUICK LEGAL NOTE:

ANY NAMES USED ARE COPYRIGHTED OR PATENTED AND ARE TO SHOW WHERE I WAS OR WHAT I USED OR OTHER AT THE TIME OF USE. EVERYTHING ESE IS FOR ME. AND ALL PICTURES NOT DRAWN BY ME—THE FACIAL CRANIAL NERVES, WERE USED WITH PERMISION, THANKS TO PATRICK J. LYNCH, A MEDICAL ILLUSTRATOR & AUTHOR, I'VE BEEN WORKING ON THIS FOR A WHILE AND THE TROUBLES JUST CONTINUE.

I REMOVED MOST REAL NAMES BUT WILL RELEASE LATER IF I DO GET CANCER OR IF A DR. REQUEST THE REAL NAMES, THEY ARE ALL MAJOR DRUGS I USED, ALL STATIN DRUGS HURT MY HEALTH AND I DID NOT WRITE EVERY PILL IN HERE, JUST PUT THE MOST OF IT. MY STOMACH STAYS RAW AND BOTHERS ME ALL THE TIME, PAIN EVERY DAY, AGAIN MORE PAIN AND MORE SPOTS I DID NOT KNOW COULD HURT. JUST HAD MORE TEST DONE THIS NOV. 2011, LOOKING INSIDE MY BLADER, PAINFUL. I WILL ALSO NOTE, THE PEOPLE I TALKED TO I TOLD THEM IF I WRITE BOOK 2, THEY WILL GET TO TELL THERE STORY IN FULL LIKE MINE, I KNOW I TAKED TO 600 EASY THAT I SEE ALL THE TIME AND MORE I RUN INTO OFTEN.